D1281571

VIRGIL AND JOSEPHINE GORDON
MEMORIAL LIBRARY
917 North Circle Drive
SEALY, TEXAS 77474

CHAPLIN,
THE MOVIES,
& CHARLIE

VIRGIL AND JOSEPHINE GORDO
MEMORIAL LIBRARY
917 North Circle Drive
"474

Books by David Jacobs

MASTER PAINTERS OF THE RENAISSANCE

MASTER BUILDERS OF THE MIDDLE AGES

CONSTANTINOPLE, CITY ON THE GOLDEN HORN

BEETHOVEN

AN AMERICAN CONSCIENCE:
WOODROW WILSON'S SEARCH FOR WORLD PEACE

ARCHITECTURE (WORLD OF CULTURE SERIES)

CHAPLIN, THE MOVIES, & CHARLIE

CHAPLIN, THE MOVIES, & CHARLIE

BY DAVID JACOBS

Illustrated with picture portfolios

HARPER & ROW, PUBLISHERS
New York   Evanston
San Francisco   London

CHAPLIN, THE MOVIES, & CHARLIE
Copyright © 1975 by David Jacobs
All rights reserved. No part of this book may be used or reproduced in any
manner whatsoever without written permission except in the case of brief quota-
tions embodied in critical articles and reviews. Printed in the United States of
America. For information address Harper & Row, Publishers, Inc., 10 East 53rd
Street, New York, N.Y. 10022. Published simultaneously in Canada by Fitzhenry
& Whiteside Limited, Toronto.
Library of Congress Catalog Card Number: 75-6291
Trade Standard Book Number: 06-022782-6
Harpercrest Standard Book Number: 06-022783-4

This book
is dedicated to
ALBEN LEAH JACOBS
a Charlie Chaplin fan

"She's surrounded me"

Contents

Author's Note

This is not strictly a biography. A couple of perfectly fine biographies of Chaplin are available, and Chaplin himself has written his autobiography. This is, rather, the story of how an exceptionally gifted man, working in a practically brand-new medium, created a comical little character who may have made more people laugh than any other fictional character in all history. It is, in other words, the story of an artist, an art form, and a work of art.

To many writers, research, though satisfying, is not nearly so pleasurable as writing. This book, however, was like none I've ever written before: not only did it require more research than the others, but the research was pure joy.

One of the things that made it a joy was the Lincoln Center Library of the Performing Arts in New York. In the Library's main reading room is just about every good book ever published about the movies. As I went from book to book, looking up Chaplin's name in the index, I often found myself wandering far from the immediate subject and reading for hours about some of the colorful people who were the pioneers in the development of motion pictures. From time to time I had to remind myself that I was not writing about the whole history of the movies. But generally, having reminded myself, I said, "Who cares?" and read on. Eventually I was glad I had. For while such books as *My Father, Charlie Chaplin* by Charles Chaplin, Jr., and *My Life With Chaplin* by Lita Grey were helpful, they were no more so than biographies of and memoirs by such Hollywood figures as Mack Sennett, Francis Marion, Mary Pickford, Marion Davies, and the countless others whose lives touched Chaplin's, and whose experiences gave me a picture of the movie industry in its early years.

The Lincoln Center Library also has a research room where photographs, out-of-print books, and old documents of all kinds relating to the performing arts are carefully preserved. Here I was able to learn about Chaplin and his work, in reviews and articles that appeared when his films were first released. With the generous help of the librarians, I handled and studied old scrapbooks and diaries of people in the movies who may have met Chaplin. It is hard not to get buried in these wonderful memory-books. And it is even harder, afterward, to leave the Library and readjust to the 1970s outside.

But most of my research was done at the movies. I saw all of Chaplin's films, and the ones I decided to discuss in detail I saw several times. The full-length pictures were no problem—they are shown frequently enough in New York—but some of the shorter ones were tough to see. I was fortunate enough to meet a gentleman who owns prints of most of Chaplin's short works, and who was generous enough to project them for me as often as necessary. He asked me not to identify him, but I am, of course, enormously grateful for his help.

I saw the full-length features more times, really, than I had to: *The Gold Rush*, eight; *City Lights*, eleven; and *Modern Times*, thirteen. More often than not, my daughter, Alben, went with me. Indeed, it was Alben's enthusiasm for Chaplin—she was seven when the big Chaplin revival of 1972 hit New York—that gave me the idea for this book. And her memory, which is better than mine, was a great help while I was writing it.

It is a nice feeling to enjoy something worthwhile with your own kid, but it's an even better feeling to learn from your own kid. It wasn't only Alben's memory that helped me to learn about Chaplin; it was also her solid observations and insights. Alben and I went to so many Chaplin movies together that somehow I managed to pick up the ability to see him through her eyes. And through her eyes, not mine, I realized how incredibly beautiful the art of Charlie Chaplin is.

I am grateful to Charles Spencer Chaplin for making those movies. But I do want to thank Alben, too, for she, in a substantial way, was my collaborator on this book. I was just a wordsmith and go-between; all I did was type it up and take it to Elaine Edelman, a really extraordinary editor, who gave it back a couple of times just to make sure I did justice to Alben's insights.

Most of the direct quotes in this book, unless otherwise identified, are from *My Autobiography*, by Charles Chaplin.

David Jacobs, New York, 1975

CHAPLIN, THE MOVIES, & CHARLIE

1

The Most Familiar Figure

At the end of November, 1913, a twenty-four-year-old English-man named Charles Spencer Chaplin boarded a train in Kansas City, Missouri, for a trip to California. Although he was a smallish, shy, soft-spoken young man who kept to himself and had a delicate and rather serious look about him, Chaplin earned his living by being funny. Until the night before, in fact, he had been a comedian in an English "music-hall" show that had been on tour in the United States. Now, however, he had given up the stage. Now he was heading west to try to make good in a new branch of show business—motion pictures.

Early in the trip Chaplin dreamed of fame and glory in his new profession. Then he began to worry. Perhaps he had been foolish to give up his good job. Motion pictures were so new and risky. They might prove to be a passing fad, or he might prove to be unsuited to them. And if he did not succeed, he would find himself alone and unemployed in a foreign land. As every mile of railroad track brought him closer to his destination—and took him farther away from England—his uncertainty grew and his confidence dwindled.

By the time he reached Los Angeles, Chaplin had worked himself up into a dreadful mood. He was so filled with doubts and fear that he had trouble reporting for work. On the day he was supposed to begin, he took a trolley car to the Keystone Studio, paced back and forth on the sidewalk across the street, then went back to his hotel. The next day he did the same thing. On the morning of the third day, his boss telephoned to find out what was keeping him. After mumbling some vague excuse, Chaplin mustered up his courage and, at last, went to work in the movies.

Shortly after his arrival at the Keystone Studio, Chaplin created a character of his own to play on film. He was a funny little fellow with a painted-on mustache, a waddle-walk, and a cane. His clothing was formal—the clothing of a gentleman—but it was ill-fitting and in tatters; the pants and shoes were many sizes too large; the cutaway jacket was too tight, and the derby hat too small. Although Chaplin played other characters as well during his one year with Keystone, he returned more and more often to this little fellow.

Almost all of Keystone's movies were comedies, and the many talented players who worked for the studio were the best-known and best-loved film comedians of the period. Chaplin made thirty-five Keystone Comedies; when he left after only a year, he was the studio's most popular star.

In his second year in motion pictures, Chaplin wrote and directed all his own films for the Essanay Studio. Before the end of that year the little fellow he created had become, by far, the best-known figure in all movies.

Within three years of his nervous arrival in California, Chaplin was being spoken of as much more than a movie star. Discovered first by the children of the United States, his films attracted people of all ages, all classes, all interests. Serious critics, intellectuals, and theater people were almost as quick as the children to appreciate Chaplin's greatness. This was a time when people in the arts did not take motion pictures seriously at all, and yet one of the most respected actresses of the day wrote that Chaplin was "an extraordinary artist, as well as a comic genius."

Less than four years after Chaplin had paced the sidewalk across from the Keystone Studio, afraid to go in, the little fellow he played was so well-known that people all over the world called him by his first name alone. He was Charlie, or Carlos, or Charlot, or Carlino, or Carlitos: "the most familiar human figure in the world."

As one writer put it, Charlie Chaplin was "the first man in the history of the world of whom it can be truly and literally said that he is world famous."

Time passed. Chaplin slowed down. He made fewer and fewer movies, then no more movies at all. Charles Spencer Chaplin grew old. But Charlie, the little fellow on film, the wonderfully mischievous, innocent, graceful, acrobatic character with the magical gestures and the marvelously expressive face, remained ageless on film, making people laugh for generation after generation.

Charlie is still making people laugh. Today many of Chaplin's short movies are shown on television, and his full-length features are frequently revived in movie theaters. Children wear Charlie Chaplin sweatshirts to school and decorate their rooms with Charlie Chaplin posters, and rarely are they asked, "Who is Charlie Chaplin?" Sixty years after Chaplin worried whether he was making a mistake by quitting the stage, college students write papers about his films. There are more books about the man and his work on bookstore shelves today than there were when his movies first came out. He is still making people laugh, and unless the human race somehow loses that special quality known as a sense of humor, he will be making people laugh for countless generations to come.

And so it was a good thing that Charles Spencer Chaplin overcame his fears in December, 1913, and went to work in the movies. It was a good thing for him because he became rich and famous and was able to spend his life doing work that he loved. It was a good thing for motion pictures, for Chaplin was one of the screen's first true artists; he helped to make movies respectable—and profitable. It was a good thing for the millions of people who have been entertained by his films; they have had themselves some hearty laughs and, just as important, they have seen in the funny adventures of the little fellow on screen a reflection of their own struggles to live a decent life in an unfunny world.

It was a good thing, too, for the future, for all the yet-to-be-born moviegoers who will laugh at Charlie Chaplin in another age. For like all great works of art, Chaplin's best movies say something about the world and the period in which they were made.

3

Chaplin stated his messages clearly and in a way that everyone could understand and appreciate. In the future people who wish to learn something about the twentieth century will surely include Chaplin in their studies. As Gilbert Seldes, one of the first serious film critics, put it, Chaplin was "destined by his genius to be the one universal man of modern times."

Charlie's figure first appeared on screen in 1914, but not until the following year did he become a work of art. For, from the beginning of 1915 onward, the artist, Charles Spencer Chaplin, was in complete charge of all the motion pictures he made.

Once Chaplin was on his own, he revealed an interesting attitude toward himself and his work. Most of the time a Chaplin movie would be introduced with the words, "Charlie Chaplin in . . ." and then the title. After the title came the line, "Written and directed by Charles Chaplin."

Charlie and Charles: think of the different impressions the two names make. Charlie is casual and friendly, the more playful of the two. Charles is more formal and serious. Using both forms of his name may have been Chaplin's way of telling his audience not to confuse him, the film-maker, with that funny little fellow up on the screen.

And of course they were not the same. Charlie was a fictitious character, a clown. Charles had created him with a costume and makeup and a lot of imagination. Charles could turn him on and off as easily as he could control a mechanical toy. Even beyond that—beyond the fact that Charles lived in the real world and Charlie existed only on the screen—there were great differences between them. Charles was handsome; Charlie was funny looking. Charles kept to himself; Charlie would go almost any place, any time, looking for adventure. Charles was to be a film-maker for more than fifty years; he did his job carefully and knew just about everything there was to know about his work. Charlie had countless jobs—baker and farmhand, street sweeper and prize-fighter, janitor and factory worker, to name just a few—but he seldom held a job for more than a few hours a day, and he usually bungled it. Charles became a millionaire; Charlie remained penniless. Charles had only a few close friends and more than a few

4

enemies; Charlie was adored by millions of people all over the world.

They were different, but it would be a mistake to say simply that Charlie, the comical little fellow, was merely a character whom Chaplin, the writer-director-actor, created and portrayed many times. The relationship between the two was much closer than that; it was the relationship of an artist and his work.

People often wonder what well-known figures were "really like." In the case of great artists, they were "really like" their work. You may read that the great composer Ludwig van Beethoven was personally obnoxious or that the painter Vincent van Gogh was so disturbed that it was impossible for anyone to be around him for long. Yet Beethoven was not "really" obnoxious, nor was van Gogh "really" impossible, for, through their work, they inspired others and gave all mankind a chance to share the artists' sublime vision of the human soul.

Indeed, in the long view, the details of an artist's personal life are important only to the extent that they help to explain his art. Charles Chaplin made eighty motion pictures, and he played the little fellow known as Charlie, or the Tramp, in all but a handful. Charlie was the greater part of the life's work of Charles. They can no more be separated than Beethoven can be separated from his symphonies or van Gogh from his paintings.

The expression "two sides of the same coin" applies to Chaplin and Charlie. They are the same size, shape, and color, but each side contains a different image, different information, a different style. You can't see both sides at once, but you know for a fact that the unseen side is there. Most important, the coin is of one piece, cast from a single hunk of material.

This is an important thing to keep in mind as you watch Charlie on the screen or read about the life and personality of the man who created him. They look different, and they act differently, but way down in the depths of their selves, Charles and Charlie were two sides of one coin, equal parts of one whole man.

And why not? Charles and Charlie were made of the same stuff; their backgrounds were identical; they started out together. Indeed, they shared a childhood.

2

An Obscure and Shy Little Boy

In the childhood of one of the funniest men who ever lived, there was not much to laugh about. Chaplin was, in fact, a pitiful child —hungry most of the time, lonely much of the time, and disappointed time and again.

He was born in London on April 16, 1889, the son of Charles Chaplin, senior, and Hannah Hill. Both of his parents were entertainers in England's popular music halls. A music-hall show was a vaudeville, or variety, show. Singers, dancers, and comedians were the main performers, but there might also be acts by magicians, jugglers, and acrobats. Charles, senior, did a little of everything in the shows. Hannah was a singer. Both were very talented, but both had problems that stood between their talent and success.

The senior Chaplin's problem was drinking. Sometimes he got so drunk that he forgot to show up at the music hall in time for the show. Eventually his reputation for missing performances made it hard for him to get work. That, in turn, made him drink more. One day he left home and did not come back; he simply disappeared, leaving Hannah alone with her two little boys. Charlie was one year old at the time; his brother Sydney was four.

Hannah Chaplin's problem was laryngitis. After her husband left, Hannah could not afford to rest her voice for a couple of days when she felt an attack of laryngitis coming on. So she sang in spite of it, and often her voice cracked in the middle of a song. Music-hall audiences were brutal; when they did not like an act, they would boo and call out insults and sometimes throw things. As Hannah's laryngitis worsened, she became the frequent target of this abuse. Music-hall owners heard about her condition, and she had more and more trouble getting work. Soon she was playing only the shabbiest music halls, where the pay was lowest and the audiences were most cruel. Because she could no longer afford to pay baby-sitters, she had to take Sydney and Charlie to the music halls with her. It was a terrifying experience for the two youngsters—standing offstage, hearing their mother's voice crack, watching the audience laugh at her and insult her and strike her with balls of crumpled up paper.

The last such experience occurred when Charlie was five years old. As pathetic as the experience was, Charlie learned something from it that he would never forget. He learned that the same human beings who were capable of unspeakable cruelty were also capable of great kindness. It was a lesson he would teach much later in some of his films.

It happened at a place called Aldershot. Hannah's voice cracked during a song, and the commotion from the audience was so great that Hannah could not continue. When she left the stage, the manager said that he would not pay her. Hannah protested: she was willing to finish her song, she explained, but the audience wouldn't let her. The manager suggested a compromise. He had heard little Charlie singing backstage and thought he had a nice voice; if the boy went on in her place, she would be paid. Hannah agreed. The manager took Charlie out on stage and introduced him. Charlie sang a song called "Jack Jones" in a cockney English accent. The audience was delighted with the boy's spirited performance and showered the stage with coins. Charlie loved it, and so he sang and danced and clowned some more. At one point he did an imitation of his mother singing an Irish song. He had heard her voice crack while singing it so many times that he thought the song was supposed to be sung that way. When he made his voice break, the audience went wild with laughter and applause; more and more coins fell on the stage. Now Hannah walked out onto the stage to get Charlie, and this time the audience gave her a tremendous ovation.

7

The audience's first response to Hannah's voice trouble had been cruel. Charlie's imitation of her disability, though innocent, had also been cruel. And yet somehow that cruel joke, which the audience laughed at, had warmed the audience's heart. Somehow that cruelty resulted in applause for Hannah and in lots more coins.

That was Charlie Chaplin's first appearance as a performer, but it was also Hannah's last. There was no more work available for a singer without a voice, and life for her and her sons steadily grew tougher. They moved from one tiny apartment to another, each cheaper and more gloomy than the last; meals became fewer. The boys danced in the street for pennies, but they could not live on pennies. Hannah took in sewing, but because she could not make the weekly payments, her sewing machine was taken away. Then there was no money coming in at all.

Unemployment insurance and welfare were unknown in those days. In England the only alternative to starvation was a workhouse. A workhouse was not much better than a prison. You were given cheap food and a roof over your head, but you had to work hard and for no pay. Children and parents were separated and allowed only brief visits with one another. Rules were many and strict. A grown-up who broke them was thrown out to starve; children who broke them were beaten with a cane or birch.

In 1895, penniless and desperate, Hannah Chaplin took her two boys to a workhouse to live. Life there was a horror for Charlie. He contracted ringworm, and once he was unjustly flogged. But there were two kinds of pain, much worse than physical pain, that tortured him for the rest of his life. He would in fact deal with both kinds years later in his movies.

One was the pain of separation. Charlie adored his mother, and she loved him; he and Sydney were also extremely close. But at the workhouse they were all separated. Charlie was only six, and the pain of being away from his mother and brother was almost unbearable.

The other pain was more subtle; it was humiliation. Twice a week the workhouse children left the workhouse for walks. Charlie despised being stared at by the people they passed. He learned that some people seem to like feeling that they are better than other people. Even the poorest people they passed felt better than the workhouse kids; the workhouse kids were the bottom of the heap.

The only positive memory he took away from the workhouse was of learning to write his name—"Chaplin." Charlie liked to write it and to look at it. "The word fascinated me," he recalled, "and looked like me, I thought."

The pain of separation and the humiliations of the workhouse were hardest on Hannah, who suffered a nervous breakdown. She was taken to an insane asylum, leaving her sons lonelier and more miserable than ever. After Sydney and Charlie had been in the workhouse about a year, however, the authorities located Charles Chaplin, senior, and ordered him to take the boys to live with him.

Life with father was not much of a life either. Chaplin was pleasant enough when he was sober, but he wasn't sober very often. And when he was, he was usually away on tour, performing. The boys were left to the care of a woman named Louise, with whom Chaplin was living at the time. A heavy drinker herself, Louise was disagreeable at best and cruel at worst, sometimes locking Sydney and Charlie out of the house at night.

Fortunately, Hannah was soon released from the asylum and took her sons to live with her in a one-room flat in a London slum. The tiny apartment was next to a pickle factory, and at the end of the street was a slaughterhouse; the smells were unpleasant and constant. There wasn't much money, but more than before; Chaplin, senior, sent a little money each week, and Hannah again took in sewing. For Charlie, though, life was wonderful: he was with his mother again. After what he had been through, their slum reunion was like heaven.

An incident occurred on this slum street that made a strong impression on Charlie. Every day sheep were led down his street to the slaughterhouse. One day one of the sheep escaped and caused quite a turmoil. The men trying to catch it kept tripping over one another, and the sheep kept slipping out of their grip. The whole scene was quite funny, and Charlie laughed with delight. Eventually the sheep was caught. As it was returned to the slaughterhouse, Charlie suddenly realized what would happen to the sheep. "They're going to kill it! They're going to kill it!" he cried to his mother. He thought about that scene often. In his autobiography he wrote that this incident may have been the one through which he learned that comedy and tragedy often overlap.

Charlie went to school briefly when he was eight. For the most part he didn't like it. Shy and quiet, he had never had the chance to learn how to make friends, and so he was something of an outcast. To make matters worse, he had a peculiar way of talking. Actually, it wasn't peculiar at all, merely theatrical. Both of his parents were theater people; he had spent much of his life among actors, and Charlie had picked up their theatrical way of speaking. But to his cockney schoolmates, Charlie's refined speech must have seemed phoney, and they made fun of it. So Charlie talked as little as possible.

Something good did happen in school, though. Charlie had memorized a comical little story called "Miss Priscilla's Cat." One day during recess he recited it to a classmate. The teacher overheard and asked Charlie to recite it to all the children. They loved it and told other kids; the next day Charlie was asked to recite the story to every class in the school. Suddenly school became wonderful. "From having been an obscure and shy little boy I became the center of interest," he wrote.

Charlie left school gladly when he was nine. His father knew a man named Jackson who ran a troupe of vaudeville dancers called the Eight Lancashire Lads. A new boy was needed in the act, and Chaplin suggested his son. Charlie was happy because he had always wanted to be a performer.

Charlie got a great deal out of his experience as one of the Eight Lancashire Lads. Not only did he learn to dance, but he studied the acts of other vaudevillians and imitated their routines. He learned a lot about comedy and acrobatics and even became a pretty good juggler. He liked traveling from music hall to music hall and living with theater people. After several months, however, he developed asthma, an illness that makes breathing painful and difficult. Although he eventually outgrew the ailment, it ended, at least for the time being, his theatrical career.

In 1899 Charlie's father died. Almost immediately the deepest poverty returned to Hannah Chaplin's home. Without Chaplin's ten shillings a week, Hannah could not make ends meet. Hoping to relieve some of the pressure on her, Sydney took a job as a bugler on a passenger ship. Charlie, aged ten and asthmatic, tried a series of jobs: janitor, newsboy, flower seller, printer's helper, toy maker. Sometimes he did well but was fired when it was discovered that he was underage. Once he answered an advertisement for a glassblower. He entered the oven-hot factory, put his mouth to a blowing tube, blew—and passed out. His willingness to try anything was a quality he would give to the character he created many years later for the movies. And like the jobs of the little fellow on screen, Charlie's just didn't work out.

Hannah buckled under the pressure of these new hard times. Once again she suffered a nervous breakdown and had to be returned to the asylum.

Now Charlie was alone—utterly, absolutely alone. Unwashed and uncared for, he wandered the slum streets of his London neighborhood until late at night. He took odd jobs when he could find them; he stole food when he could not. He avoided his landlady—avoided everyone, for he was ashamed of his poverty, ashamed of his mother's condition, and ashamed of himself for being ashamed. He had no way of knowing that the life he was leading was providing him with experiences and emotions that he would someday reconstruct in his great art. Had he known, he probably would not have cared. At the time, probably, he would have traded the art of his future for a healthy mother and a daily life that was not a daily ordeal.

After several awful months, Sydney came home. It was a good thing for Charlie that he did. Without Sydney, Charlie—never one to make friends easily—would have had no one to talk with, to open his heart to, to dream with, to share his grief and responsibilities with. Without Sydney, the twelve-year-old boy might have become hard and cynical, too grown-up too soon. Without Sydney, Charlie would have had no one in the world to trust. For

Sydney and Charlie were much more than brothers; they were each other's best friends.

A month or so after Sydney's homecoming, Charlie received a postcard from Blackmore's theatrical agency asking him to come in for an interview. For a couple of years now Charlie had been stopping at Blackmore's from time to time to see if any juvenile acting roles were available. Now, apparently, one was.

Charlie was enthusiastic about the interview, but he was also terrified. He wanted to go on the stage with all his heart, but he was afraid that he would be asked to audition by reading from a script. At this point in his life he could hardly read! Luck was with him that day. No one questioned his claim that he was fourteen years old (although he was in fact only twelve and small for his age). And the producer and author of the play were impressed with his personality and his family's theatrical background. They gave him a part without asking him to read. He was cast as Sammy in a new play, *Jim, the Romance of a Cockney*. Best of all, Charlie was told that if he did well as Sammy, he would be cast as Billie in *Sherlock Holmes*, a major play scheduled to go on a forty-week tour beginning in the fall.

Charlie raced home with the script of *Jim*. When Sydney heard the news, his eyes filled with tears. He was sure, Syd said, that this was the turning point in their lives. There wasn't much time for celebration, though. Sydney had to read Charlie's lines to him over and over again until Charlie had memorized them. Three days later Charlie had the part down pat.

Sydney's feeling was right. Charlie stepped into the role of Sammy and out of the nightmare that had been his childhood. It had been a bleak period in his life, and it left him a shy, brooding youth, slow to trust others, better acquainted with the sadness of life than with its joys. But it also gave him an understanding of what it means to survive.

3

The Vaudevillian

With his role in *Jim, the Romance of a Cockney*, Charlie began his show business career in earnest. Except for a few short layoffs while he was a teenager, he was never again unemployed.

Jim, however, was just a stepping-stone to his really big break, the part of Billie in *Sherlock Holmes*. As a play, *Sherlock Holmes* proved to be as popular as the wonderful mystery stories about this brilliant detective. It was a first-class production with fine actors, and when the company went on its forty-week tour, theaters in cities and villages throughout the British Isles were packed. So successful was the tour that after it was over, the producers arranged a second tour of the same duration. And this time there was a small part in it for Sydney, who also proved to be an accomplished actor.

During the second tour Hannah Chaplin was judged well enough to leave the asylum. The happy Chaplin brothers found a lovely London apartment for her and for themselves when they were in town. Sadly, Hannah soon suffered a relapse and had to be returned to an institution. Although much later the boys were able to afford the best doctors for their mother and would bring her to California to spend her last years in luxury, Hannah never regained her full mental faculties. Indeed, she was never even lucid enough to understand that her younger son was a world-famous celebrity.

After *Sherlock Holmes* the Chaplin brothers went to work for music-hall companies. Unlike many performers, Charlie and

Sydney did not think that straight dramatic acting was in some way more artistic than playing vaudeville. (That attitude, which their father held, was so widespread that the theater of traditional drama had come to be called the "legitimate" theater—a term that suggested that vaudeville was illegitimate.) Charlie and Syd loved the spirited, fast-paced music-hall shows. Both had a flair for comedy and knew that the English music hall was the perfect place to develop their comedy talent. They could not get jobs with the same company, however; so they split up and found work where they could.

Sydney's success came more quickly than Charlie's. One reason was Syd's age: he was a mature-looking eighteen when the *Sherlock Holmes* tour ended, and Charlie was a youngish and awkward-looking fifteen. Another reason was Sydney's greater—or different kind of—discipline. Syd was a hardworking trouper who followed directions carefully and practiced the conventional music-hall routines (called "bits" or "bits of business" by players) until he had them right. Even at this young age, Charlie was not good at following directions. He was much more likely to experiment, to try new approaches to comedy, and to devise his own bit of business. In his own way, of course, he was extremely disciplined. But his discipline was that of an artist: he drove himself to invent, to be original, to revise and refine his work until it was perfect. The road to perfection was bumpy. The music-hall producers saw young Charlie bouncing over the bumps. Syd's course was much smoother.

At that time the producer of England's best music-hall shows was Fred Karno. In 1906 Karno spotted Sydney Chaplin performing with a small company and signed him to a contract. Although Syd soon rose to become one of Karno's leading comedians, he could not convince the producer to take a look at Charlie; Karno thought that Charlie was too young. In 1907, however, Karno lost a player and told Sydney to send for his eighteen-year-old brother.

"He wasn't very likable," Karno said, recalling his early impression of Charlie. "I've known him to go whole weeks without saying a word to anyone in the company. . . . On the whole he was dour and unsociable. He lived like a monk, had a horror of drink, and put most of his salary away in the bank as soon as he got it."

Onstage, though, Charlie was funny, and his boss was pleased. After the young comedian displayed his talents in a number of secondary roles, Karno offered him the leading part in a brand-new show. The show, called *Jimmy the Fearless*, was typical Karno fare. It wasn't a play in the usual sense of the word, but neither was it a succession of unrelated acts. It was, rather, a vaudeville show with a sketchy story or "theme." In this play Jimmy is a good-for-nothing youth who displeases his parents and is sent to his room, where he reads a Wild West thriller. He falls asleep and has a series of incredible dreams, all set in the old West and in which he is always a hero. Each of the acts in the show is related to these dreams: the dancers are cowboys; the singer of sweet songs is placed in a saloon setting; and the comedy skits are somehow adjusted to fit the theme. Other Karno shows—*The Football Match, Jail Birds, His Majesty's Guests*, and many more—had very similar acts, but the changing themes brought freshness to old routines and inspired the players to think up new ones.

Astonishingly, Charlie appeared indifferent to Karno's offer; he didn't seem to care whether he got the lead in *Jimmy the Fearless* or not. Perhaps he was just in a bad mood, or perhaps he suffered a sudden loss of confidence, but whatever the reason, his attitude annoyed Fred Karno. Understandably, the producer withdrew the offer and gave the part of Jimmy to a more eager newcomer, Stanley Jefferson. Soon after, though, Charlie's ambition returned, and he became a valued member of the Karno troupe.

(Incidentally, Stanley Jefferson, a slim, sad-faced, and wonderfully kind young performer, later followed Charlie Chaplin's example and migrated to the United States to make a career in the movies. He changed his name to Stan Laurel and teamed up with a fat, rosy-faced American named Oliver Hardy. And Laurel and Hardy did very well indeed.)

Karno's shows were first-class entertainment, vaudeville at

its best. They were always carefully rehearsed and beautifully presented. The Karno players took great pride in their work. They respected and studied each other's talents. They complimented one another, criticized one another, taught one another, and kept the standards of the whole company high. In this atmosphere Charlie Chaplin became a professional in the best sense of that word.

In English vaudeville, comedy was king. Comedy was very important in American vaudeville, too, but not in the same way. At its very best, an American vaudeville show was a more even balance of acts—songs, lavish dances, and short comedy skits. English vaudeville came out of different traditions, the ancient traditions of clowning and pantomime.

Pantomime is an art that stands somewhere between dancing and acting. A mime—one who performs in pantomime—tells a story silently, with gestures and the movements of his body. The European tradition of pantomime goes back to the early days of the Roman Empire. Governed by a set of ancient rules, traditional, or "classical," pantomime survives to this day, especially in France and Italy. Marcel Marceau of France, the most famous practitioner of the art, is a "classical" mime: he never speaks during his act, and he very often works alone.

But the pantomime of the English music hall was not classical. The Karno players were not mimes in the traditional sense; they studied pantomime to learn to make their gestures and movements as expressive as possible. Pantomime was not something to be mastered for its own sake; it was a tool to be applied to the fast, furious, physical, knockabout kind of humor their audience loved—the humor known as "slapstick." Moreover, the English vaudevillians usually worked as a group. They loved even their most rough-and-tumble, seemingly haphazard "bits of business" to have a certain rhythm and harmony. Learning pantomime, with its dancelike grace, helped them to maintain those qualities.

The tradition of European clowning was also absorbed into the training of Karno's troupe. The "deadpan" clown is another ancient fixture in European entertainment: he is the clown that just stands there, expressionless and reactionless, as thousands of mishaps rain upon him. There is a trace of pathos—the quality that arouses sympathy from others—in the performing of most great clowns, and that quality seems to make the clowns' performances a little sadder and a little more funny at the same time.

All of Karno's players were skilled English-type mimes and clowns, and their performances were popular not just in England, but in France and the United States, where their technique was quite unusual. In 1910 Karno sent a music-hall troupe to the United States for a nationwide tour, and among the company he sent was Charlie Chaplin.

The Karno show was a huge success in America, but it returned to London smaller than when it had left. Karno had lost some of his best players—not to American vaudeville, but to the infant branch of show business known as motion pictures. It seemed that the emphasis on pantomime and on fast and rhythmic action characteristic of English vaudeville was terrific training for players in movies.

In 1912 Fred Karno was asked to send two troupes to the United States. He wanted to oblige, for the American tours were very profitable, but he was afraid that he would lose more performers to the movies. After giving the matter some thought, he decided to send the two companies, but to keep his best players at home. Accordingly, Sydney Chaplin stayed in London, and Charlie—who had come back from the 1910 tour—was shipped across the Atlantic.

Before he left England, Charlie reassured his boss that he would return home. He just couldn't imagine himself, he said, being funny in front of a camera.

Charlie was the star of the Karno show called *A Night in an English Music Hall*. As its name suggests, it was typical English vaudeville—but it was more. It was a show-within-a-show, designed to give Americans not only a look at English vaudeville but also a taste of the music-hall atmosphere.

England's music-hall audiences were not shy about expressing their opinion of a show. Not all audiences, however, were as brutal as the one that had shouted Hannah Chaplin off the stage at Aldershot. In the better London music halls, where the entertainment was generally first-rate, the show was more likely to be interrupted by one or two rowdy persons than by all the patrons. These individuals, who were called "hecklers," did not necessarily dislike the show. Often they were drunks; occasionally they were just people who thought themselves as funny as the comedians onstage and wanted to show off. Sometimes, when the heckler really was funny, the comedians would answer him. They'd shout back and forth, each trying to top the other in insults.

The boisterous audience and the heckler were as much a part of English vaudeville as the ballad singer. Therefore, in Karno's *A Night in an English Music Hall*, a stage was built on the stage of the theater. A small "audience" of Karno players sat in seats in front of the smaller stage and in a fake box seat to one side of and over the smaller stage. This pretend-audience shouted and stomped and heckled and gave the show its authentic music-hall flavor. And, best of all, since they were carefully rehearsed and talented comedians, they gave it the flavor without the annoyance; for real hecklers, nine times out of ten, weren't funny at all.

The main heckler was Charlie Chaplin. Dressed in a tuxedo and top hat, pretending to be drunk, he sat in the box over the stage and watched the show. He couldn't find a thing to like about it. After each act and during a few acts, he shouted out his displeasure. He and the players traded insults; sometimes their argument would get so heated that he would start to climb down out of his box to fight. Usually he would be persuaded to climb back in, and that, for a man in his "drunken" condition, wouldn't be easy. His backside stuck way out; he'd slip and slide upward, almost falling a dozen times, until finally he'd make it back into the box, where he might take a loud-snoring snooze until there was another act to insult.

Chaplin was a very important part of the show—its leading player, really—since he was onstage not just during a few acts but through the entire performance. After his first heckling early in the show, the audience constantly looked his way, waiting for his next outburst. It was a hard role. His timing had to be perfect: he had to time his interruptions so that each one came

Charlie

KEYSTONE CHARLIE: 1914   During his first
year in motion pictures, Chaplin learned the business,
experimented, and created the costume and many
of the tricks of the comical little figure known as Charlie
or the Tramp. This roguish Charlie, tailored to the
frantic style of the Keystone Comedies, was a master of
the arts of darting, ducking, chasing, and being
chased. He starred in thirty-five movies at Keystone,
becoming the most popular comedian in motion pictures.

Charlie meets the motion-picture camera—and
doesn't think much of it—in *Kid Auto Races.*

Charlie and Ford Sterling
in *Between Showers*.

Tillie (Marie Dressler) catches husband Charlie
with Mabel Normand in *Tillie's Punctured Romance*.

Chaplin's first film under his own control
had a fitting title: *His New Job*.

In *A Night Out*,
Charlie and Ben Turpin
spend every minute
smashingly drunk.

Charlie steals hot dogs in *In the Park*.

THE "REAL" CHARLIE: 1915   In complete charge
of his own movies, Chaplin began to create a more
complex character. The new Charlie was more innocent,
and sometimes he was incredibly sad—an unusual
emotion for film clowns in the early days of movies. But
Charlie still had his share of vices. He would lie to
get work. He went on occasional drinking binges. And
when he was hungry, he saw nothing wrong with
stealing his dinner.

In *The Champion*, Charlie's pathetic look
is shared by his bulldog friend, Spike.

Charlie's drinking problem drives him
to a sanitarium in *The Cure*—only, he
can't stand the cure itself.

Charles Spencer Chaplin,
author, director, and star
of some of the funniest
movies ever made. But in
person Chaplin
(here in his twenties) was a shy,
sensitive, and serious young man.

At the conclusion of *The Tramp*—for the first but far from the last time on film—a disappointed Charlie walks alone down life's long, lonely road.

as a surprise to the audience, which was difficult because the audience already expected him to interrupt. Furthermore, each interruption had to be completely different from the previous one—unless, that is, the audience was expecting a completely different one; in that case it would be funny only if it were the same. It was a hard role, but Chaplin played it well. He was complimented by reviewers, and his performance made a good impression on a man who had an especially good eye for comedy talent.

The man's name was Mack Sennett, and his Keystone Studio in California made motion pictures.

There is some disagreement about when and where Sennett first saw Chaplin perform. According to some accounts he saw him during the 1910 tour; others have it that he saw *A Night in an English Music Hall* during a New York trip early in 1913. Whatever the case, Sennett did nothing at the time, but he recalled the Englishman's performance in the spring of 1913, when he thought he might be needing a new comedian for his Keystone Comedies.

In May, 1913, a telegram came to the Philadelphia theater where the Karno troupe was playing. It was an inquiry: Was there "a bloke called Chapman, Caplin, or something" with the company? If so, would he please call on Mr. Charles Kessel in New York? Kessel was one of the owners of the New York Motion Picture Company, which owned—though Chaplin didn't know it at the time—the Keystone Studio.

"Chapman, Caplin, or something" could mean only Chaplin.

The twenty-four-year-old vaudevillian from England took a train to New York and met with Kessel, who offered him a job in the movies. After a little negotiation they agreed on terms: a one-year contract at a weekly salary of one hundred and fifty dollars.

Chaplin returned to Philadelphia to complete his tour with Karno's troupe. The tour ended in Kansas City on November 28, 1913; the next day he left for California. And the rest, as they say, is history.

4

The Movies: Keystone Comedy

When Chaplin began his long career in film-making in 1913, motion pictures were still very young. The date generally given for their beginning is 1889—coincidentally, the year of Chaplin's birth. In that year Thomas Edison invented the kinetoscope, a box with a peephole on top and a crank on the side. The viewer put a penny in a slot and turned the crank and saw a "moving picture" of a bit of action, perhaps only a minute long. In 1895 two French brothers, Auguste and Louis Lumière, invented the *cinématographe*, the first machine to project a motion picture onto a screen. Almost as soon as news of this system of projection spread, motion-picture companies began to form, especially in the United States. The earliest movies, like the kinetoscope shows, recorded action—the finish of a horse race, the knockout in a prizefight. But before long pioneers were experimenting with and expanding the use of film equipment, and the contents of motion pictures steadily became more complicated.

In France a magician named George Melies astounded audiences with his "magic" shows on film. Today we take motion-picture effects for granted, but in 1900 many of these effects did seem magic to audiences. Some of Melies's most popular "tricks" were performed by inanimate objects, such as a row of chairs. In one film Melies had the chairs begin to quarrel and then fight with one another. To film this was easy: all Melies did was to photograph the row of chairs, turn off the camera, move the chairs a little so that one seemed to "nudge" another, turn the camera on and off, tilt the "nudged" chair against the next chair, turn the camera on and off, and continue this procedure until all the chairs were involved in the brawl. When the film was projected, the chairs appeared to move. (The same principle is used in the filming of an animated cartoon, which is made from a series of drawings.) Melies's "magic" showed other film-makers how versatile film could be: much more than just the recording of bits of action could be done with it.

In 1902 in the United States, Edwin S. Porter began telling stories on film. These very first "photoplays" were not merely photographed from a stage; they were photographed in bits and pieces. Often the same performances were shot several times from different angles. Sometimes scenes near the end were photographed before opening scenes. Much more film was taken than was used. Porter invented film "editing"—the process of cutting and splicing pieces of film to tell a continuous story.

There were two main, very practical reasons why photoplays were best put together in the cutting room. One was the fact that these early movies were silent. In stage plays information was provided by means of dialogue. Motion pictures had some dialogue—words on printed titles—but too many interruptions for printed words made the photoplays very boring. Therefore, film-makers had to tell their story as much as possible with visual images. If a man's dreamy face appeared on screen and then an image of a woman and a child appeared over his head, the audience knew that the man was thinking of his family. This effect—the "dream balloon" over the man's head—had to be worked out by overlapping pieces of film. Secondly, even these very earliest photoplays were "crosscut" to show that events were happening at the same time. In Porter's 1903 film *The Great Train Robbery*, the bandits are shown escaping while a young girl discovers the telegraph operator tied up; as she unties him, the robbers are seen getting away. It would have been wasteful to set up the camera equipment to photograph the bandits, then set up the cameras again to photograph the girl's discovery of the operator, then reset the equipment to film the bandits again, then the girl helping the victim, and so forth. Much simpler was filming the whole sequence of the bandits' escape and then the indoor sequence with the girl and the operator. The crosscutting was done in the cutting room.

In 1908 the movies' first great artist, D. W. Griffith, went to work for the Biograph Studio in New York. Griffith perfected many of the techniques that have been called the "language" of film: dramatic lighting, close-ups, flashbacks, the moving camera, and scores of other devices that became basic tools of motion-picture storytelling.

Mack Sennett, who became Chaplin's teacher, learned his trade from Griffith. Sennett, born in 1880 in Canada, had been a poor, tough, uneducated youth who happened to love vaudeville. He worked as a boilermaker to earn money for tickets to the shows, and he liked the zany atmosphere so well that he taught himself to dance and got a job as a vaudeville chorus boy. But when the movies got started, he went to work for Biograph and soon was playing comic roles in D. W. Griffith's lighter movies. After he learned Griffith's techniques, he persuaded the Kessel brothers in New York to put up the money for his own studio in Los Angeles—the Keystone. And he would make only one kind of movie: comedy.

As Griffith was Sennett's teacher, so Sennett became the teacher, directly or indirectly, of Charles Chaplin and just about every film-maker who has successfully used motion pictures to make people laugh. Sennett understood film, and he understood comedy. He knew all the tricks that could be played with motion-picture photography, and he used them all. He had the ability—absolutely essential to moviemakers—to shoot a film in pieces, not necessarily in the order called for by the final story, and yet to keep his vision of the whole. Other comedy movies had been made before he founded Keystone, but Sennett developed a kind of comedy that was perfectly suited to the screen. He understood that silent movie comedy must be a skillful blend of cutting room "magic" and the right kind of performances. And the right training for such performances was the vaudeville stage, mainly because of the vaudevillians' pantomime experience. Perhaps the most important ingredient in Sennett's success was his wonderful judgment. In the cutting room he was without mercy. He eliminated hundreds of feet of film for every fifty he kept. And he used only one measure: if a gag made him laugh, it stayed; if not, out it went.

Sennett influenced all movie comedy, in the sound as well as the silent era, but there was something extra special about silent comedy. The late critic James Agee called the silent period "The Golden Age of Comedy," and many people familiar with silent comedy say that nothing else makes them laugh quite so hard.

It is hard to say what makes silent comedy so funny, but it does have something to do with silence. Dramatic movies always suffered from the lack of sound in the early years. No matter how realistic the director made his film, the drama could not ring true because an important part of reality—noise, voices—was missing. Silent comedy, though, was crazy from the word go. Since *nothing* was realistic, no false note was struck by just one more unrealistic thing. Nothing seemed missing.

Moviemaking at the Keystone Studio was very informal. Several times a week Sennett and his associates had a story conference. Any of the players and technicians who were not busy making a movie at the time were welcome to sit in and contribute ideas. As soon as a rough idea for a film was accepted—the Keystone Comedies were not shot from scripts—the necessary material was assembled. The propman got together his strange collection of items, which might typically include a giant mallet that looked like wood or iron but actually was soft rubber; some soft, felt bricks that looked like real bricks; a telephone that shot water into the face of the person using it, and maybe forty or fifty custard pies. If the movie was supposed to take place indoors, the scenery maker pushed together some screens to give the impression of a room and furnished it. If the story was to be placed in an outdoor setting, the players and camera crew would leave the studio for the nearby countryside, or—more rarely—for downtown Los Angeles. When shooting began, the "story" was established very quickly; then the players were encouraged to try any action that might be funny—the more outlandish the better, as long as the action related to the story idea. As Sennett himself explained it, "Having found your hub idea, you build out the spokes; those are the natural developments that your imagination will suggest. Then introduce your complications that make up the funny wheel." All the bits of business led to a familiar Keystone climax. This might be a chase—the Keystone Cops never needed much of an excuse to give chase: if they saw something moving, they chased it—or a colossal pileup of some old cars, or a pie-throwing scene. Most Keystone Comedies in 1914 were one or two reels long (one reel of film took between twelve and sixteen minutes to show). Most were photographed in less than a week, many in only a day or two, and some in just a couple of hours.

Keystone Comedies were completely crazy. The strangest, most impossible things took place in them. Men ran faster than speeding automobiles. Fat police officers jumped from the ground to the roofs of buildings. A custard pie soared through the air, turned around like a boomerang in mid-flight, and splattered in the face of the person who threw it. A hundred cops climbed out of one tiny car. And everything happened very fast, for Mack Sennett believed that motion pictures should have plenty of motion—constant, rapid-fire motion. To create this speed and those peculiar goings-on, he depended on lots of camera trickery.

A motion picture is nothing more than a series of still photographs taken one after another and projected so quickly that the human eye cannot distinguish between the individual photographs. Each individual photograph is one "frame." In the days of silent movies, film was photographed and projected at a speed of sixteen frames per second. At Keystone, however, Sennett told his cameramen to shoot most scenes at a speed of twelve frames per second. If a chase, for example, took one minute to enact, the cameraman would take 720 pictures. But when that film was developed and shown on a projector at the normal sixteen-frames-per-second rate, the whole scene on the screen would last only forty-five seconds. And of course when a minute's worth of action was compressed into three-quarters of a minute, all movement was greatly speeded up. (The effect can be compared to that of a

33⅓ rpm phonograph record when it is played at 45 rpm.)

As the camera could increase action to a dizzying pace, it could also create comical illusions. Suppose that a director wanted to have a car drive off a cliff into a river, bounce right back up out of the water onto the cliff-top, and continue a chase. Such a gravity-defying trick was easy to accomplish. During the shooting of the film, the cameraman photographed the whole chase except for the car's fall from the cliff, which he filmed last. After the film was developed, the editor cut it at the point where the car reached the edge of the cliff. Next he made a print of the car's fall into the river and another print of the same strip of film in reverse—last frame first, next-to-last frame second, and so on. In other words, the upward flight of the car was simply the downward fall, backward. Finally the two strips of film showing the fall and bounce back were spliced onto the rest of the film in between the first and last part of the chase.

Photographing a hundred cops getting out of a miniature car was even easier. First the camera was placed in a secure position and turned on while two actors drove the car onto the set. When the two actors got out of the car, the camera was turned off, and two more actors slid into the car; when the camera was turned back on, these players climbed out. Off went the camera, into the car went two more policemen, on went the camera, out came the cops, off went the camera. This went on and on until enough policemen had left the tiny car. When the film was developed, it contained only footage of the Keystone Cops getting *out* of the automobile. Typically, the last man out was a midget. After he climbed out, the car collapsed.

Anyone who has seen a Keystone Comedy knows how funny these photographic tricks can be. But they were not needed to make Charlie Chaplin funny. In fact, they would actually intrude on his type of humor. Nobody knew this better than Chaplin himself. And because he knew it, and because the men who were in charge at Keystone did not know it, there was trouble between the comedian and his bosses from the very beginning.

5

A Born Screen Comedian

Chaplin had been hired by Sennett to replace Keystone's leading comedian, Ford Sterling, who was going to form his own company. Sterling was still under contract when Chaplin started making movies, and Chaplin noticed that all the other Keystone players seemed to imitate him. Known as a "Dutch-style" comic, Sterling performed in a grand, overblown manner with exaggerated gestures and reactions. Hit on the head, he might stare blankly for a few seconds, roll his eyes around and around a couple of times, go limp, turn a few circles, fall to his knees, grip his head, slide down flat on his back, and bounce two or three times before losing consciousness. Such bits of business could be funny, but they were not Chaplin's style. Chaplin preferred a subtle, understated kind of comedy, closer to the deadpan style of the English clown. Furthermore, the dizzy pace of the Keystone movies struck Chaplin as unsuitable to his talent. For he felt that personality, not camera trickery, should be the basis of his comedy.

Moreover, Chaplin did not like to follow the directions of others. In his very first film, *Making a Living*—in which Chaplin appeared as a character much like the heckler in the Karno show—he and the director argued constantly. Acting as peacemaker, Mack Sennett told Chaplin that they would forget the tension of the first film and start from scratch. In fact, it might be a good idea for Charlie to get into a new costume.

There are several stories about the hour or so that Chaplin

spent rummaging through the wardrobe room at Keystone. At least six people have claimed that they first suggested the outfit that Chaplin put together to show Sennett. Chaplin himself has written that he had decided on the kind of costume he wanted by the time he reached the wardrobe room.

In any case, he decided to make himself a tramp. But he would not be an ordinary tramp: he would be a "gentleman" tramp, dressed in ragged but formal attire. He found some baggy pants and big, floppy shoes, which he put on the wrong feet. To make a funny contrast with the oversized clothing below the waist, Chaplin dressed himself with a cutaway jacket that was too tight and a derby hat that was too small. He picked up a flimsy-looking cane, and exchanged the big, villain's mustache of *Making a Living* for a smaller one that did not hide his facial expressions. Nothing in this costume was necessarily original; what was original was what happened to Chaplin once he put it on.

When Chaplin had dressed himself in his new outfit, he returned to the filming stage to show Sennett. He began to strut about, swinging his cane, winking and tipping his derby hat, and Sennett began to respond. "The secret of Mack Sennett's success," Chaplin wrote later, "was his enthusiasm. He was a great audience and laughed genuinely at what he thought funny. He stood and giggled until his body began to shake. This encouraged me and I began to explain the character: 'You know this fellow is many-sided, a tramp, a gentleman, a poet, a dreamer, a lonely fellow, always hopeful of romance and adventure. He would have you believe he is a scientist, a musician, a duke, a polo player. However, he is not above picking up cigarette butts or robbing a baby of its candy. And, of course, if the occasion warrants it, he will kick a lady in the rear—but only in extreme anger!' "

And so Mack Sennett sent Chaplin in his new getup out with the director to try again.

For this next film not even a story idea was needed. Keystone was going to film an actual event: the Kid Auto Races at Venice, California. Chaplin would simply clown around before the camera while the event took place.

Chaplin made thirty-five Keystone Comedies in 1914, most in

the role—or at least in the costume—he'd created for *Kid Auto Races*. But he never did learn how to take direction. At first Sennett tried directing Chaplin himself, but the motion-picture business was growing by leaps and bounds in those days, and the boss had to take care of the problems of expansion. Then Sennett promoted Chaplin to two-reel comedies and had the studio's leading woman comic, Mabel Normand, direct. Mabel actually was Sennett's girlfriend; she was pretty and talented, and Chaplin had a crush on her. Sennett probably hoped that the longer film and Chaplin's affection for Mabel would help create harmony on the set. No such luck: Chaplin's resistance to direction was greater than his eagerness to please the twenty-year-old Mabel, and at one point he even threatened to quit and return to England. Ever the peacemaker, Sennett made himself codirector of the film—it was *Mabel at the Wheel*—persuaded Chaplin to apologize to Mabel, and convinced Mabel to ask for Chaplin's valuable suggestions. But even with harmony restored, Sennett probably was sorry that he'd ever signed up the temperamental Englishman.

Then everything changed.

In 1914 it generally took Keystone two or three months to get a movie to the public. After the film was photographed, it had to be developed and edited. Then about twenty prints were made and packed in film cans. A distribution schedule had to be worked out in New York, newspaper advertisements placed, posters printed for display outside theaters, transportation arranged, and the canned movie shipped out. And after the movie was shown, its success or failure could not be determined for a couple of weeks more.

At this time the exhibitors—the people who owned the theaters —were beginning to be able to choose from a great many films. (Several years earlier the demand for movies was temporarily greater than the supply; by 1914 the supply had more than caught up. Hollywood was making movies faster than the exhibitors could build theaters.) To help decide which movies to book, exhibitors subscribed to several trade newspapers, such as *Moving Picture World*, *Motion Picture News*, and *Bioscope*, and the two show business papers, *Variety* and *Billboard*. These journals offered critical reviews of all the new movies, and their critics had to be good if the exhibitors were to trust their judgment.

At about the time Mack Sennett was ironing out the differences between Mabel Normand and Charlie Chaplin over *Mabel at the Wheel*, Chaplin's earliest movies were en route to their first showings in theaters around the country, and critical judgments of his playing were beginning to appear in the trade papers. The very first was printed in a favorable review of *Making a Living* in *Moving Picture World*. "The clever player who takes the role of the nervy and very nifty sharper in this picture," wrote the reviewer, "is a comedian of the first water, who acts like one of Nature's own naturals." An international movie journal called *The Cinema* perceived the impact of Chaplin's performance in a review of his second film: "*Kid Auto Races* struck us as about the funniest film we have ever seen. . . . Chaplin is a born screen comedian; he does things we have never seen done on the screen before." Of Chaplin's third film, *Mabel's Strange Predicament*, the *Exhibitors' Mail* wrote: "The Keystone Company never made a better contract than when they signed on Chas. Chaplin, the Karno performer. . . . We do not often indulge in prophesy, but we do not think we are taking a great risk in prophesying that in six months Chaplin will rank as one of the most popular screen comedians in the world. Certainly there has never been before quite so successful a first appearance."

As the first ten or twelve Chaplin movies reached the critics' screening rooms, the reviews, one after another, piled praise upon praise. It was as if the whole trade press had united to applaud the new celebrity. "We have seen seven Chaplin releases, and every one of them has been a triumph for the . . . hero . . . who has leapt into the front rank of film comedians at a bound. Chaplin has created an entirely new variety of screen comedian. . . . " "If there is an audience anywhere that does not roar when they see this comedy they cannot be in the full possession of their wits. . . . Mr. Chaplin has introduced a number of funny actions that are original to the American stage." "The person who does not laugh at the peculiar antics of Chas. Chaplin—well, must be hard to please."

The praise was not lost on the exhibitors, who began demanding more Chaplin films. By the end of April, 1914, Charlie Chaplin had leapt over every member of the Keystone troupe and become the studio's most popular star.

Actually, Chaplin, Sennett, and the rest of the Keystone players were not the first to learn of Charlie's sudden popularity. Most of Keystone's business operations—including distribution—were handled in the New York office. When exhibitors wanted more Chaplin, they told New York, not Hollywood. New York, in turn, wired California, but the message might be as brief as "Send more Chaplin quick." Such a message obviously told Sennett that Chaplin was a hit, but not how big a hit. Sennett did not know that by late spring—a mere six months after Chaplin's arrival in California—critics in the trade press were referring to Chaplin simply as "Charlie," confident that everyone in the business knew who Charlie was. (And everyone in the business did.) Nor could Sennett know right away that the New York office was increasing the price of Chaplin's movies and making greater and greater profits for the Keystone Company. The exhibitors were paying the higher prices because much of the public was beginning to know this new star as Charlie and was willing to pay more to see him. Indeed, years later, Sennett himself admitted that even at the end of Chaplin's contract year, Sennett did not fully appreciate the extent of Chaplin's popularity.

But they did know in California that Chaplin was a success, and beginning with his thirteenth movie, *Caught in the Rain*, Chaplin was permitted to conceive and direct most of his films. At first Chaplin regarded Charlie the Tramp as his main man, a proven laugh-getter to return to when nothing else came to mind. As Chaplin began turning out his own movies at the familiar fast Keystone pace, however, the Tramp, as if he had a life of his own, began to make himself a permanent fixture.

In Chaplin's first own-made movies, the comedian assumed a variety of roles. In *Caught in the Rain* he was a hotel clerk. In *A Busy Day* he played a woman. He was the bandit in *Her Friend the Bandit* and the referee in a prizefight in *The Knockout*, a dentist's assistant in *Laughing Gas* and a baker in *Dough and*

Dynamite. Yet, in each of these movies (except for *A Busy Day*), Charlie appears, when he is not on the job, in his Tramp's getup. Knowingly or not, Chaplin was creating a character who was much broader than any one individual role. In other words, he was steadily fashioning a character who was *first* the Tramp and *only incidentally* a clerk, referee, or baker.

This had an important effect on audiences. Imagine yourself a moviegoer in 1914. You go to the movies once or twice a week, and week after week you see Charlie as the Tramp. Even if he is dressed as the Tramp for only a minute or two in each film, you soon begin to feel that the Tramp's clothing is his real clothing, the Tramp's character his real character. You draw that conclusion because, after seeing Charlie in a couple of movies, you come to realize that the job he holds this week he will not have next week. This week's clerk will be next week's baker. But the character is constant; he and his Tramp's getup will remain the same. For Chaplin did not attempt to be an actor who played a variety of parts. Instead he created one character who tried to assume whatever role was needed at the moment. The audience got to know that character.

It is important to keep in mind, however, that in Chaplin's Keystone films the Tramp was just beginning to take shape. If it was true that the majority of the films made by Chaplin in 1914 were his own creations, it was also true that they were Keystone Comedies. Director or not, Chaplin was required to obey the Keystone conventions. His movies still had the frantic chases and custard-pie wars that he would give up when he left Keystone. Furthermore, the Tramp was not yet well defined in Chaplin's own mind. The early Keystone Tramp is a bit more roguish than the later Keystone Tramp. The Tramp who is a jealous husband in one film is a drunken husband in another, a henpecked husband in another, and in still another he is a wandering husband, attracted more to pretty Mabel than to his own wife. The Tramp would leave many of these characteristics—especially wickedness and deviousness—at Keystone with the custard pies.

Incredible as it may seem, Mack Sennett did not renew Chaplin's contract at the end of the year. Chaplin simply wanted too much money. Sennett was making a fortune: in the spring of 1914 he had assembled the whole Keystone cast to make his first full-length (six reels) motion picture, *Tillie's Punctured Romance*. It was released later in the year, and all signs indicated that the film was going to be the greatest money-maker in the young history of commercial movies. Signs of prosperity notwithstanding, Sennett was afraid of a salary landslide: if he paid Chaplin what Chaplin was demanding, all of the company would demand similar raises. Sennett decided to lose Chaplin.

Years later the great American film critic James Agee asked Mack Sennett how he felt, looking back, about his decision to let Chaplin slip away from Keystone. Sennett simply shrugged; he was not the kind of man who nursed his regrets. "I was right at the time," Sennett told Agee and was satisfied to leave it at that.

Agee asked Sennett what he thought of Charlie Chaplin, the man who had gotten away. Said Mack Sennett: "Oh well, he's just the greatest artist that ever lived."

6

Charlie the Tramp

When word got around that Charlie Chaplin and the Keystone Company would not be renewing their contract, the Universal Studio contacted Chaplin. No deal was completed because Universal thought that his request for a salary of one thousand dollars a week was too steep. Their failure to come to an agreement, however, started rumors in the motion-picture business. Most of the big movie studios, the rumors said, were after Chaplin, and he was demanding astronomical terms. These rumors must have frightened away some studios that otherwise might have tried to sign him. For the fact was that as 1914 neared its end, Chaplin was having some pretty anxious moments. He was a hit, but where was the stampede of studio representatives? He was the brightest new star in movie comedy, but where were all the stupendous offers? Was he going to follow in the path of Ford Sterling, whose career had been sliding downhill since he'd left Keystone? Chaplin must have wondered.

At last an offer arrived. It was made by the representative of the Essanay Company. Fortunately for Chaplin, the Essanay man had heard the rumors; he understood, he said, that Chaplin was asking for twelve hundred and fifty dollars a week plus, just for signing a contract, a bonus of ten thousand dollars cash. "This was news to me," Chaplin admitted later. "I had never thought of a ten thousand dollar bonus until he mentioned it, but from that happy moment it became a fixation in my mind." He stuck to those terms, and Essanay agreed to them.

Leaving Keystone was not easy for Chaplin. Mack and Mabel and some of the other Keystone players were among the few real friends he had ever made. Moreover, during his year at Keystone, Chaplin had persuaded Sennett to sign Sydney to a contract. Syd had come from England and become one of the studio's leading comedians. And Syd, of course, was his younger brother's one and only really close friend. Essanay's main studio was in Chicago. Going there meant leaving his new friends and brother. On his last day of work at Keystone, Chaplin could not even bring himself to say good-bye. He simply finished shooting and went home. The next morning he set out for Chicago.

Immediately after the New Year's holiday, Chaplin started work on his first Essanay film, a two-reeler entitled, appropriately, *His New Job*. The movie was a simple spoof of moviemaking; in fact it made friendly fun of the Keystone Comedies. Set in the "Lockstone" Studio, it featured Charlie as a property man and actor who destroys the set, the scenery, the costumes, and finally the movie itself in his attempts to do his job. The movie ends with a chase that wrecks the entire studio. The chase is funny in the best tradition of Keystone chases, but it is more: it is also a spoof of the Keystone chases.

After completing *His New Job*, Chaplin told Essanay that he did not like working in Chicago. Anxious to please the new star, his boss suggested that Chaplin work at the Essanay studio at Niles, California, near San Francisco. Although he really wanted to return to Los Angeles, Chaplin agreed to give Niles a try.

There were several reasons, personal and professional, why Chaplin wanted to go back to California. One was Sydney; Chaplin was lonely again in Chicago. Another was climate. Not only was California's more agreeable; it was also better for filming. But the main reason was that California was the center of the movie world: the best technicians and actors were there. Now in complete charge of all his films, Chaplin was eager to take advantage of the expert personnel and facilities available in California. Whether or not first-class services would be within reach at Niles remained to be seen, but certainly it was closer to the center of things than Chicago.

Most film-makers in the early years of the movies appreciated the value of using the same cast and crew over and over again, and Chaplin was no exception. A film troupe, like a good football team, was most efficient when its players knew one another, understood one another's strengths and weaknesses, and worked well together. He began to form a good, steady company in Chicago. While filming *His New Job*, he found one wonderful player in Ben Turpin. A skinny, long-necked, cross-eyed comedian who looked a lot like a scrawny chicken, Turpin was good—too good, actually, to remain a permanent part of Chaplin's company. After making several Chaplin films, Ben went out on his own and became one of the five or six most popular clowns of the silent film era.

When Chaplin left Chicago for the West coast, he also took along the cameraman of *His New Job*, R. H. Totheroh. The meticulous Totheroh remained Chaplin's photographer for over thirty years.

Essential to any lasting company was a leading lady. In Chicago Chaplin had not been able to find an actress with the qualities he was looking for. Continuing his search at Niles, he described the sort of woman he wanted to his Essanay colleagues. One player said that he knew of a young woman who might be suitable. When Chaplin located her in San Francisco, he was a little disappointed. Her looks were right—she was very beautiful, soft and sensitive looking, and naturally elegant—but she seemed so sad and serious that he doubted that she could ever act with humor. Nevertheless, he hired her. She would be, as he put it, "decorative," and she would serve as a temporary leading lady until someone better came along.

Her name was Edna Purviance, and she was nineteen years old. After he hired her, Chaplin would make forty-four more films. Edna Purviance was his "temporary" leading lady in thirty-four of them.

Edna was very important to the development of the Tramp. She played many roles—including a nagging wife and a rich, spoiled young debutante—but most often she was a sweet and innocent type, a girl who stirred the Tramp's protective instincts.

Edna's presence changed the Tramp and added a new dimension to his film character: she gave him a goal to reach for. Sometimes the goal was attainable, sometimes not; but as he strove to reach it, he become a symbol of the little man trying to protect an island of innocence and find a little happiness in the middle of a corrupt and cruel world. The characteristic relationship between Edna and Charlie began to take shape in their fifth movie together, *The Tramp*.

The Tramp was shot in Los Angeles. After shooting four movies at Niles, Chaplin complained that he could not work as well there as in southern California. Essanay had a shabby studio in Los Angeles that could be renovated, and the film company was willing to undertake the expense.

In *The Tramp* the little fellow that Chaplin was creating would reveal, for the first time, all of his dimensions. In his previous movies the Tramp develops as a comical and often cunning figure filled with contradictions. He is a tramp in a gentleman's clothing, shabby but formal. He is usually a vagabond, but he has the flawless manners of a dandy. He is not a bum—he certainly isn't lazy—for he is willing to tackle any job. But he seldom does the job properly. His enemies are figures of authority and objects. He is not always completely virtuous: in *A Night Out* he and Ben Turpin spend the whole two reels smashingly drunk. He is not always completely honest: as a boxer in *The Champion* he knocks out his opponents by placing an iron horseshoe in his glove. He is not a commonplace rascal, however, because he has a conscience, an aspect that began to emerge in the Essanay films. His heart of gold is demonstrated in the opening scene of *The Champion*. Half-starved, Charlie has gotten hold of a frankfurter, which he sits down to enjoy. Just as he is about to take a bite, he sees that his little friend, a bulldog, is gazing hungrily at the piece of meat. Charlie can't bear it and lets the dog have the first bite.

But *The Tramp* contains something not present in the earlier films: the ability to arouse sympathy in others. Without this pathos, Charlie had been funny, but with it he became much more. He became tragic as well as comic, and therefore more fully rounded, more real. He became a figure with whom people in the audience could identify. The trials, ambitions, and frustrations of the little fellow might be exaggerated, but they nonetheless symbolized the trials, ambitions, and frustrations of all ordinary little people.

In *The Tramp* Charlie demonstrates two characteristics that will stick with him throughout his life on screen. One is his habit of falling in love. The other is his ineptitude. Early in the film he rescues Edna from a gang of vagabond thieves who attack her as she counts her savings. In gratitude, Edna, a farmer's daughter, takes Charlie home, and her father gives him a job as a farmhand. Among the chores Charlie is given are watering the trees and milking the cow. Charlie does not explain that he is a city boy and knows nothing of such things, but he is determined to figure out how to do them. After taking a beating at the handles of various rakes, hoes, and spades, Charlie finds a small garden watering can and fills it with water from the hose. (Of course it is the hose that he should use to water all those trees, but he doesn't realize that.) And with this tiny watering can he proceeds to water the orchard. Now he looks at the cow. His head tilts and his mouth twists and he rubs his chin in thought. Let's see . . . how to do this. Aha! He puts a bucket under the cow's udders. So far so good. And now he walks behind the cow, takes hold of its tail, and pumps! Oddly enough it doesn't work. He's confused. That's how a pump works; why shouldn't a cow work the same way?

During the night, while Charlie is asleep in the barn, the thieves try to break into the house. Charlie awakens and calls out, rousing the farmer and frightening away the criminals. Followed by the farmer, Charlie chases after them; the farmer fires his rifle, and Charlie is struck in the leg by the bullet. The injured hero is returned to the house and cared for during a long recovery by the devoted Edna. Charlie mistakes Edna's gratitude and devotion for love, and he is glad because he is falling more deeply in love with her every day. He lives for her daytime visits, and at night he dreams of the two of them, and their children, in a lovely home on their own farm. Weeks pass, and Charlie feels that his leg is better. Alone, he gets out of bed and goes to the window; his leg is fine, it seems. But when he reaches the window, he looks out and sees Edna in the arms of a young man, her lover. Charlie's heart is broken. He gathers his things together and leaves the house, tipping his hat to the empty kitchen as he goes. He finds Edna and says good-bye, smiling. Are you sure you're all right? her gestures ask; wouldn't you like to stay a little longer? No, Charlie pantomimes; I've been here too long; I've things I must tend to. They part, and Charlie begins his walk down a long, dusty road into the distance.

You can see from *The Tramp* why Edna was such an important element in the development of Charlie. It is her part that gave Charlie the opportunity to develop the quality of pathos. In this and future movies Edna is a sweet, loving young woman. Her devotion to Charlie is genuine; her rejection of him is unintentional. She is so modest that it does not occur to her that he loves her. She is such a good person that Charlie takes special care, when he realizes the truth, not to let her know that she has hurt him. He knows that she would be terribly upset if she knew. He does not want her to feel guilty; he does not want her to feel anything but happy. He does not want her sympathy because that would cost him the most wonderful of all his traits, his dignity. For the Tramp never loses his dignity, no matter what.

His dignity is displayed beautifully in another Essanay film, *The Bank*. When Charlie arrives in the morning at the bank where he works, he carries himself with a great show of importance: he is as pompous as the bank president. Inside, he goes directly to the vault, and with all the solemnity required by so important an act, he opens the combination lock. When the gigantic vault door opens, Charlie removes his coat, hangs it up, and reaches into the vault for his mop and pail. He is, alas, the janitor, though he is the most dignified man in the bank.

He even manages to retain that dignity when, as usual, the objects he works with turn against him: it is clear that his mop hates him, and the various doors in the bank consider it their duty to be precisely where his chin happens to be heading. During his ordeals with his object-enemies, Charlie finds the time to worship, from afar, his co-worker, Edna. Here again, as in *The Tramp*, Charlie is doomed to disappointment, for Edna is in love with the bank's cashier. Brokenhearted at the discovery, Charlie retreats to a corner and slumps down, dejected. Then, suddenly, bank robbers appear and lock Edna in the vault, but Charlie foils the crooks and rescues his love. Now Edna sees the real hero in Charlie. They embrace—and Charlie finds himself kissing his mop. It has all been a dream. At the moment when he awakens, Edna is kissing the cashier. With a sigh he picks up his bucket and mop and goes back to his work.

The public loved this new Tramp. Even critics who had previously thought Chaplin too slapstick and silly joined the ranks of his admirers. From coast to coast and in Europe, a Charlie Chaplin poster outside a movie theater meant a full house inside. Charlie Chaplin dolls and statuettes went on sale in department stores and drugstores. The beautiful women in the chorus of the famous Ziegfeld Follies in New York painted little mustaches on their faces, wore baggy pants, imitated Charlie's movements, and danced while singing a song called "Those Charlie Chaplin Feet." And none of this was lost to the careful eye of Sydney Chaplin.

When Syd's contract expired at Keystone, he decided, at his brother's urging, to devote himself to Chaplin's business affairs. Although the younger Chaplin had good instincts when it came to matters of money, Syd was a brilliant businessman: he could negotiate as shrewdly as the best lawyers and was a sort of financial wizard. With Sydney in control of the money, Charles Chaplin became one of the three or four richest figures in show business.

As Chaplin's contract year neared its end, Essanay tried hard to re-sign their star. Although they offered generous terms, they were, for some reason, unwilling to agree to one of Chaplin's demands: that he receive a bonus of one hundred and fifty thousand dollars for signing a contract. Knowing how valuable his brother had become, Sydney would not dicker. He boarded a train for New York, and within a few weeks he concluded a deal with the Mutual Company. Chaplin got his cash bonus—plus a salary of ten thousand dollars a week. A total of six hundred and seventy thousand dollars for a year's work!

The twelve movies Chaplin made for Mutual and the fifteen he made for Essanay are, collectively, a sort of series, during which the fully rounded Tramp appears, develops, matures.

Charlie the Tramp is definitely not a bum. Throughout his life on film he is employed more often than not, and the trials of working are almost as consistent a theme in his movies as the tribulations of loving. Charlie wants to work, is eager to please, and gives every new job his full attention and enthusiasm. His performance, however, usually falls short of his desire. Sometimes it is his boss who gives him trouble. Charlie's boss is typically crude and humorless; he expects and demands a great deal but is unwilling to teach; he thinks that Charlie, with his delicate manners and dignified bearing, is crazy. Charlie's attempts to ingratiate himself are ridiculous and only make the boss more suspicious.

Sometimes inanimate objects are the source of Charlie's trouble. Throughout his life on film the Tramp carries on a running war with *things*. In Charlie's hands objects seem to have lives and wills of their own, and their aims are always sinister. Wet mops in Charlie's possession feel solemnly obliged to slap him or his boss in the face every time Charlie spins around. Ladders are determined to cuff him around the shoulders. Handles of farm or garden implements sincerely believe that Charlie's face is their punching bag. All the world's folding furniture has entered into a solemn agreement never to set up properly for him. Sometimes objects get him so confused that he loses all sense of which are which. He is known, on occasion, to put his cane to bed and tuck it in and go stand himself in the corner; when he gets thirsty he picks up the telephone and pours himself a glass of water.

Actually, compared with some other film comics, Charlie's wreckage record was pretty good. The Keystone Cops were quite capable of reducing anything to rubble, and that tradition lasted straight through the Golden Age of Comedy. Destruction was an art in the hands of Laurel and Hardy; many of their funniest movies were written to build up to a scene in which everything handy—be it a house or a hundred cars in a traffic jam—would be wrecked. Charlie's destructiveness was more subtle and was almost always a result of his ineptitude.

In *The Pawnshop* Charlie displays ingenious skill—or ingenious ineptitude—handling an ordinary alarm clock. A man brings in the clock for repair, and Charlie, a clerk, takes a look. With all the concern and finesse of a surgeon, he listens to the clock with a stethoscope, tapping the side as if it were a human chest. When all this delicacy yields no diagnosis, he tries another technique—and pries the clock open with a can opener. Then, using anything handy—dentist's tools, a hammer, and an oilcan—he dissects the poor clock, examining every part under a magnifying glass, pulling the mainspring out straight and measuring it. A little spring drops on the counter and wiggles about; Charlie oils it till it stops. That'll teach it! By now the clock is nothing but a heap of tiny scraps. Charlie takes the customer's hat and puts all the pieces inside. He hands the man the hat and shakes his head sadly. Yes, you're right, his expression says, it doesn't work.

The clock-wrecking sequence in *The Pawnshop* is one of Charlie's funniest scenes, and it demonstrates that destruction does not have to be on a large scale to be very effective. And for the most part Charlie continues his war with objects in that small but fierce way.

Charlie is not much kinder to his own body than he is to inanimate objects: his life is filled with bumps and falls and collisions. His rear end never lacks for exercise. When Charlie carelessly throws a banana peel to the ground, he just as carelessly becomes its first victim and lands splat on his prat. When Charlie is employed as a waiter, there is no way for him to carry a tray of food from the kitchen to the table uneventfully; even if the food does arrive intact, it must have passed through a number of detours and near-disasters en route. For Charlie and mishaps go through life together like a bee and honey; where there is something to trip over or stumble into, Charlie is sure to find it.

But when he does find it, he turns it into something glorious. Because Charlie is a wonderful natural dancer whose movements lead gracefully from one to the next, even his banana-peel pratfall is executed with the smoothness of a ballet step. The whole sequence of his movements is one continuous dance movement, planned and executed with graceful precision.

Many of Charlie's funniest experiences are choreographed. (Choreography is the art of creating and describing the dancers' movements in a ballet.) *In the Park* (1915) is an old vaudeville comedy routine redone with such precision that it turns into a dance. A thief and Charlie pick each other's pockets at the same time; both are disappointed. Charlie then goes off and steals some franks from the hot-dog man, while the thief steals Edna's purse. Then, while the thief steals Charlie's hot dogs, Charlie steals back the purse. The snitching goes back and forth until, at the end, Charlie finds himself confronting Edna's beau and chased by the thief, the hot-dog man, and a passing policeman. A well-placed kick here, a step-aside there, and Charlie, like the Pied Piper of Hamlin, drives the rats one by one into the lake. That taken care of, he turns his attention to the wooing of the lovely Edna. It is all very funny, but it is all so smooth and precise that the viewer is carried along by the rhythm as well as by the humor.

Chaplin's careful choreography could turn the simplest or most routine bit of business into a thing of beauty. In *The Floorwalker* (1916) Charlie the Tramp comes face-to-face with his look-alike, the floorwalker in a department store. Their resemblance is so marked that at first each thinks that he may be looking in a mirror. Each moves his arms together, each scratches his head in confusion; each reaches forward to touch the fingertips of the other. They seem to be reflections, but neither can be sure. Finally Charlie notices that the other holds a satchel instead of a cane, and the confusion is set straight. (Many years later the Marx Brothers did their own version of this routine in their movie *Duck Soup*.) The joke is simple, and the movements of the two men are minimal, but as a funny dance the sequence is a miniature jewel. The same movie ends with a chase down the up escalator of the department store. The comedy built into a moving stairway is obvious to almost everybody. Almost all of us have made ourselves laugh by taking a few steps in the wrong direction on an escalator. But Chaplin's perfectly timed choreography takes the obvious and makes it new. Charlie stops to take a breath, and the stop is almost disastrous, taking him back up closer to his pursuers; a churning of his feet takes him down again; he slips and falls getting off, and the stairs take him back up. Only Charlie could turn so obvious a routine into so graceful a dance.

Charlie's clumsiness is graceful, but he also uses his astonishing agility to save the day. In *The Adventurer* (1917) Charlie is an escaped convict who tries to lose his captors by mingling in the crowd at a fancy party. One of the waiters opens a bottle of champagne, and Charlie, thinking the *pop!* a gunshot, immediately puts up his hands in surrender, almost giving himself away. But he instantly realizes his mistake and cleverly converts the gesture into one of smoothing down his hair. At the end of the movie, while Charlie apologizes to Edna for disrupting the party, a prison guard finally grabs him. Without a split-second's pause in his movements, Charlie courteously introduces the guard to Edna. The introduction is so natural that the guard automatically responds: Why, how do you do, gestures the guard with his outstretched hand. Of course that had been the hand that had held Charlie. It doesn't anymore, and off Charlie goes.

7

Chaplin the Celebrity

Chaplin was so busy, working so hard, that he hardly had time to notice the two strangers rushing up behind him. One day he turned around and there they were: Wealth and Fame. Suddenly he was a rich celebrity. And never would he be anything else again.

It was too much to understand, especially the money. Chaplin never saw the money—Sydney took care of it for him—and the sums were so great and multiplied so fast that they were meaningless to him. Not that he didn't care for it; he did. As Sam Goldwyn, the pioneer movie producer and a friend of Chaplin, once put it: "Charlie is no businessman—all he knows is that he can't take anything less." But the astronomical amounts he demanded—and got—were really symbols to Chaplin in the early years, proof of his success. He didn't see them as money, exactly, as something to be spent.

When he left Karno in 1913, Chaplin had been earning a salary of sixty dollars a week. In those days a young man of his modest tastes—and who had so recently known such deep poverty— was able to live quite comfortably on thirty or forty dollars a week. His one-year contract with Keystone called for a salary of one hundred and fifty dollars—a fortune! A year after that he was getting a thousand a week from Essanay—and still living a forty-dollar-a-week life. Then ten thousand a week from Mutual, not to mention the one-hundred-fifty-thousand-dollar bonus. And finally a contract with First National Pictures: eight comedies for one million two hundred thousand dollars.

But what did it mean to him? A great deal, of course, for the knowledge that he was rich was a great comfort to a formerly poor boy. But it scarcely affected his life-style. For a Hollywood celebrity, Chaplin lived very simply. He was certainly no socialite. He enjoyed an occasional party if the host was a friend—his closest friends at this time were Douglas Fairbanks and Mary Pickford. He liked prizefights, and he was very enthusiastic about good vaudeville, which he attended once a week. (In Chaplin's opinion the greatest entertainer on the American stage was Al Jolson.) But for the most part he lived simply and spent a lot of time alone. Acutely aware of the fact that he had almost no formal education, he became a constant reader, concentrating especially on philosophy. He also enjoyed good music and even took violin lessons.

Since his work demanded that he keep in top physical condition, Chaplin went regularly to the Los Angeles Athletic Club, where he rented a bedroom to relax after his workouts. One day late in 1917, after a bath, he was lolling around his room at the club, a towel around his waist, playing a piece from *Tales of Hoffman* on his violin, when Sydney appeared. Chaplin's contract with Mutual would expire soon, and Syd had been busy negotiating with various studios for a new agreement. Chaplin was now, Syd told him, officially a millionaire. "I suppose that's wonderful," Chaplin said and continued playing. Syd burst into a laugh. He'd always remember that picture, he said: Charles in a towel, playing the violin, and his ho-hum reaction to a deal worth one million two hundred thousand dollars for only eight two-reel movies.

But mainly he worked. He worked so hard that he really didn't have the energy for a flamboyant life: he was simply too tired at the end of the day.

Still, wealth was indeed a great comfort to him because it drove one of his life's demons—poverty—away from him for all time. Not only was it wiped out; it was erased quickly and quietly and painlessly, while his back was turned, while he was doing his job.

His other demon—loneliness—was not so considerate.

Chaplin had often been lonely as a child. Small and sensitive, he really loved only two people, his brother and his mother. The circumstances of his life, combined with his delicate size and temperament, made it difficult for him to fit in with others or to trust others. His family had survived on its own, with little help from anyone. Sudden wealth and fame were not enough to turn him suddenly into a person who could reach out to people and share himself with them.

He and Sydney learned very young to depend only on each other. In his autobiography Chaplin is very kind to and understanding of his father. Yet there can be little doubt that his father was a disappointment to him. Charles, senior, abandoned his family, after all, and when he was located, although he was agreeable enough himself, he turned the boys over to the care of a bitter, unpleasant woman. He then drank himself to death, leaving his boys alone again. No, Charles, senior, was no one to reach out to or look up to. So Charles and Sydney never learned the habit of reaching out or looking up, and clutched instead at each other.

Indeed, Chaplin learned, very early, that the best way to face up to the outside world was to hide his real self in a performance. The little boy, watching terrified as a bunch of rowdies insulted his mother at Aldershot, had turned the brutes into an affectionate, generous army. How? By pretending he didn't hate them, by smiling and singing and dancing. By making them laugh. The same boy, a little older, a friendless loner in a slum school, had made himself a special person, the center of attention. How? By reciting a silly story. By reciting it well. By making his schoolmates laugh. And again, a couple of years later, the same boy got himself a job on the stage. One can almost see him in the office of the theatrical agent, twelve years old, a miniature version of the character he would create in the movies. No mustache, of course, but that familiar shy smile would be there and the twinkle in the sad eyes, perhaps even the same swinging leg as he sat on the edge of the desk, using his expressive face and body to make himself seem relaxed and confident instead of scared stiff.

And getting the job because he'd been entertaining. And then the theater jobs, the end of hunger and worry. And how did he get rid of the hunger? By performing. Everything good that had come to him, it seems, had come because he had entertained. What lesson had he learned from all this? Hide yourself, put on a mask, make people think that the mask is you, make them laugh. Since that had been the only formula that had worked for him, that was the formula he stuck with.

He had always loved his mother; he adored her. She was so beautiful and delicate and affectionate; once she had been so talented. But she had been destroyed. The things that had destroyed her art and her mind were things that could not be touched or destroyed in return. His poor, pitiful father had hurt her. Then fate hurt her, or whatever it was that took her songs away. Then the society that took away her sewing machine and shoved her and her two boys into a workhouse, a hell on earth. She had been a religious woman in her way—not a churchgoer but a believer in faith and prayer. When all else had gone, she retained her religious faith, and in Charlie's mind that faith had let her down. He never liked religion. He thought of her when he thought of it. It was something she had held on to through all her trials, and when it hadn't come through for her, its failure was just one more disappointment. Perhaps it had been the final disappointment, the one she couldn't bear, the one that drained her mind of hope and reason.

By the time he was a grown man she was beyond help. He brought her to California and visited her and showed her movies in her fine seaside home, but all he could do was make her comfortable. He would have liked to protect her and share his good life with her, but it was too late.

He had loved another woman once. Her name was Hetty Kelly, the sister of one of the fellows in the Karno troupe. He was nineteen when he met her; she was several years younger, pretty, lively, and flirtatious. Chaplin was terribly shy: he'd wait for hours in the park near her home and "accidentally" run into her, and they'd take a walk or stop at a teahouse. But he was unable to let her know how he felt, and Hetty never took him seriously.

47

Actually, Chaplin never did get over his shyness with women. He didn't have to. If he never learned how to flirt or make advances to women, it may have been because women flirted with him. By then he was Charles Chaplin, and he was rich and famous, very handsome, and only in his twenties.

He did not like worldly, sophisticated women. The quality he was most drawn to was innocence—a quality contained in almost all the women characters he created in his movies. In the movie world that Chaplin entered in 1914, there was no shortage of very young women—girls, really. Early motion-picture photography was crude; it tended to make shadows look darker and deeper. This had the effect of making players appear to be considerably older on film than off. As a result, most of the actresses of the period were very young—a fifteen- or sixteen-year-old was right to play the part of a woman in her early twenties. These actresses were not innocent little girls; they were hardworking professionals in a tough, competitive business. Nevertheless, being as young in years as they were, many did have the fresh, unspoiled, girlish look that Chaplin was attracted to. He often seemed to be sadly disappointed to discover that the girl he was so eager to protect and share a first love with didn't need protection and had loved before.

Women came to him, and he took them; but he didn't have any serious love affairs, though he was always looking for one.

He might have found it with Edna Purviance, but luck was against them. When Chaplin went with Essanay in 1915 and hired Edna, she was nineteen, a wholesome, blonde, smooth-skinned woman who photographed young. More often than not the part she played in Chaplin's films reflected the sort of girl Chaplin—and Charlie—idealized: soft, sweet, innocent, and trusting.

Away from their work Chaplin and Edna became almost inseparable. Offscreen Edna was no china doll to be protected and preserved; she was a mature woman who had a mind of her own and a will as strong as Chaplin's. But that was all right, because neither wanted to get too serious too soon. Both were young, good-looking, and famous, and both wanted to enjoy their popularity and freedom before settling down. Chaplin in particular was having a splendid time. He who had had to lurk around like a criminal just to look at Hetty Kelly was now the target of a hundred Hetty Kellys.

In 1917, when he was twenty-eight, Chaplin began seeing a fifteen-year-old actress named Mildred Harris. Mildred was, in appearance, everything that Chaplin adored: small, soft, and exquisite. After a courtship of several months, they married. Chaplin was not sure marriage was a good thing for them even as they wed, but he really wanted a home and family, and he tried to make it work. So did Mildred. But before long they knew they were unsuited to one another. They were divorced in 1920.

The real tragedy of his marriage to Mildred Harris—and Chaplin admits as much in his autobiography—was not that the marriage failed. They had no children, and the divorce was handled without bitterness. The real tragedy was that it ended the romantic relationship between Chaplin and Edna. In the back of both their minds had always been the thought that they would marry someday. When Chaplin suddenly married Mildred, that possibility disappeared forever. The scar was too deep ever to heal.

Chaplin's marriage to and divorce from Mildred Harris was the subject of considerable publicity. Like all Hollywood stars, Chaplin was a public figure, and whatever he did was news. Chaplin never adjusted to this role. He was, in fact, a private person, a shy man who liked to be—and seemed to need to be—alone.

It was not easy for a public that adored Charlie to understand how very private Chaplin was. Many people tend to think that celebrities should behave a certain way just because they are celebrities. Wealth and fame, of course, influence their personalities but do not change them into completely different human beings. Like everyone else, Chaplin was formed by his childhood. By the time he started his career in the movies, he was twenty-four years old—an adult. Wealth and fame did not instantly transform him into someone else.

In his autobiography Chaplin himself tells a story that reveals how little success changed the inner man. After two years in the movies, Chaplin had to go to New York on business. By this time he was the screen's most famous figure. In Hollywood he had been pursued by some of the most beautiful women in the country, and he was at this time deeply involved with two of the very loveliest, Edna Purviance and Mildred Harris. Certainly this handsome, rich, and famous young man should have gained confidence by now. While in New York he heard that his secret first love, Hetty Kelly, was living with her sister in that city. He found the address and walked to the house. But when he got there, he did not have the courage to call. Instead, he walked back and forth in front, hoping that Hetty would come out so that they could "accidentally" bump into one another. He was one of the most famous men in America, but he was still no different from the shy young Karno trouper who had arranged accidental meetings with Hetty Kelly in London years before.

Chaplin never overcame that shyness, and he remained, for the most part, a loner. To some extent the speed and size of his success may have helped to keep him that way. For unlike many people who achieve great fame, Chaplin never had the chance to learn how to be a public figure. One day he was a comparatively obscure vaudevillian, and almost the next day he was world famous.

And as soon as he was world famous, he was, for one reason or another, under some kind of attack. He responded to the attacks the only way he knew how: by not responding, by keeping quiet. His refusal to respond irritated his enemies, who attacked even more. When finally he had no choice and had to respond, he responded honestly. He never learned how to avoid sensitive subjects. And in the times in which he lived, sensitive subjects were plentiful.

One sensitive subject was Chaplin's nationality. When World War I broke out in Europe in 1914, some people thought that Chaplin should have returned to England to fight for his country. When the United States entered the war in 1917, some Americans wondered why Chaplin hadn't become an American citizen and enlisted in the American army. For his part Chaplin did help in

50

By 1916, when Chaplin made *The Vagabond*,
Charlie's mournful expression was as
familiar to moviegoers as his funny faces.

A natural choreographer, Chaplin gave Charlie the grace of a ballet dancer. Here nimble Charlie skates in *The Rink*.

Charlie and Eric Campbell, the villain of many early Chaplin films. This is a posed studio photograph.

"Doctor" Charlie examines his "patient"—an ailing alarm clock—in these stills from *The Pawnshop*. No surgeon ever operated with a greater sense of style.

THE STYLISH BUNGLER: 1916-1917   Charlie may be inept, but he botches each job with true grace and proper form. One of Chaplin's consistent themes is society's attitude toward manners—the silly idea that it doesn't matter much what a person does, so long as he looks right doing it. The banker's pompousness, the policeman's bullying, the salesperson's fake courtesy were among the many postures that Charlie mastered and mocked.

In *Easy Street,* Officer Charlie gasses a gangster into submission with an unusual weapon—a corner gaslight.

Charlie as
The Floorwalker:
and oh, that poor
department store!

Charlie and his beautiful leading lady,
Edna Purviance, in *The Immigrant*.

MORE TO SAY: 1918-1919   With *A Dog's Life*
and the remarkable *Shoulder Arms*, Chaplin gave Charlie
a little more room to show off his growing complexity : these
films were three reels instead of the usual two (a reel was
twelve to fifteen minutes long). When they were completed,
Chaplin knew that he had mastered the ability to tell
stories that were sad and funny at the same time.

In *Shoulder Arms* (1918), Charlie,
posing with perfect pomposity as a
World War I German officer, rescues Edna.

That pathetic face again:
Charlie and his pal
Scraps in the sad-and-funny
A Dog's Life (1918).

Charlie's exquisite dancing was at its
peak in the dream sequence of *Sunnyside* (1919).

Chaplin, in Charlie's costume, poses on the lot of
his studio with his brother, best friend, and
business adviser, Sydney Chaplin, around 1920.

the Allied cause: he made a film to sell war bonds, and he traveled around the country with other movie stars, participating in rallies that raised a great deal of money for the war effort. Like many other entertainers—and indeed like the Allied governments themselves—he felt that lifting the morale of the people and getting them to support the war was his best way of contributing.

After the war some Americans continued to resent Chaplin's refusal to apply for United States citizenship. Chaplin did not feel very strongly about citizenship one way or another. Like many intellectuals, he thought that patriotism did as much harm as good. Moreover, he considered himself a citizen of the world, and if anyone in this century had a right to call himself that, who more than Chaplin? He did not wish to make national citizenship an issue at all; if he were to give up his British citizenship in favor of American, wouldn't that be making an issue? Leaving things alone was the best way, he thought, to express his indifference to the subject of national identity. And besides, he could always point out that leaving things alone was a reasonable compromise: he retained his British citizenship, but he paid his enormous taxes to the United States.

It sounds like simple logic now, but Chaplin's refusal to become an American citizen haunted him for years.

8

Citizen, Soldier, Work of Art

In 1915 Chaplin had made fifteen movies for the Essanay Studio;
in 1916 and 1917, under contract to the Mutual Company, he
made a total of only twelve. Most of these movies were two reels
long; so it is clear that Chaplin was working at an ever slower
pace. He was not, however, becoming less productive. Indeed,
he was working harder and harder, taking more time and care
with each film. By the end of his fourth year in motion pictures,
he was ready to create works of art. He had the know-how, and,
even more important, he had the subject: Charlie.

Like many another artist, Chaplin had profited from a youthful
period of trial and error. He may not have liked the hectic pace of
moviemaking at Keystone, but it had forced him to experiment
and improvise and learn his craft. In a sense his year with Sennett
had been his education, the studio his "art school." And when he
graduated, he had a sketchbook filled with preliminary images of
Charlie. This little fellow in the sketchbook already looked like
Charlie, waddled like Charlie, and had many of Charlie's habits
and gestures. He could skid around a corner on one foot, his other
foot extended straight out, while he held on to his hat. He even
had much of Charlie's mischief. But he was not quite yet the
legendary Charlie.

Working on his own from 1915 onward, Chaplin began to model
his Charlie character more intricately. The Essanay and Mutual
films are not rough sketches; they are more like fine drawings in
charcoal or pen and ink, most of them suitable for framing. In

these movies Chaplin detailed all the special qualities of temperament that make Charlie Charlie. His devotion and loyalty. His yearning for respectability. His loneliness and longing for romance. Most important, Chaplin now created a three-dimensional character, a complex fellow with real depth. Like all interesting human beings, like all great works of art, Charlie is more than he appears to be. He looks like a tramp, but he has the manners of a gentleman. He sleeps in haystacks and doorways, but he fastidiously cleans his fingernails before every meal. He is kind and trusting, but he is known to give a fellow worker a swift kick in the seat of the pants if the occasion calls for it. He is a loner, but he can also be a good, dependable friend. He is incredibly naive, but if necessary he can outsmart the shrewdest wise guy.

The three-dimensional Charlie who first appeared in *The Tramp* revealed his many sides to moviegoers in the series of films released by Essanay and Mutual in 1915 and 1916. During those two years Chaplin was content to use Charlie's character as the main theme of his movies. By placing Charlie in a different situation in each, the artist was able to cast different lights on his subject. Once the subject was well defined, however, Chaplin, like any conscientious artist, wished to enlarge his themes. He wanted to develop more complicated circumstances in which his three-dimensional character could be used to make statements not just about himself, but about the times and society in which he lived. Thus, as Chaplin completed his contract with Mutual with four films in 1917, the social themes in his work became stronger.

Society confuses Charlie. He is not a bad citizen, exactly, but he does have a little trouble being a good, law-abiding citizen. The pillars of society—policemen, ministers, community leaders—say that they dispense equal justice to all, that they wish every man to pursue happiness in his own way. In practice, however, they seem to want something else. As Charlie travels from adventure to adventure, he finds that men are judged not by how virtuous they really are, but by how respectable they seem to be. He finds that a place in society is earned with money, not goodness. He finds that society does not really want people to be themselves but to conform—to act the way that society expects them to act.

He finds a big difference between the picture society paints of itself and the reality that society creates.

In *Easy Street* Charlie, down at the heels and starving, enters a mission for a meal. The minister and the beautiful organist, Edna, take an interest in him and give him an inspiring talk on the rewards of Christian piety. Charlie is so moved by their talk that he immediately returns the collection box, which he had stolen on the way in. Then the do-gooders give him another inspiring talk, this time on the rewards of good citizenship. Charlie is so moved that he joins the police force. Assigned to Easy Street, which is being ravaged by gang war, the rookie cop comes face to face with the local bully, who demonstrates his strength by bending the post of a gas lamp to a right angle. Charlie, being Charlie, doesn't let the opportunity pass: with one swift gesture he spins the bent lamppost around, fits the gas lantern over the bully's face, turns up the gas, and gasses the bully into unconsciousness. Later the bully escapes from jail, and Charlie recaptures him by dropping a stove on his head. In another scene Charlie is overpowered by a crook and accidentally falls onto the hypodermic needle of a dope addict. The narcotic works on him the way spinach works on Popeye. Afraid of nothing, Charlie whips his enemy and pacifies all the neighborhood gangsters. When the dope wears off, his reputation lingers, and thanks to Officer Charlie, peace prevails on Easy Street.

Easy Street is satire: it makes fun of the way society evaluates its members according to a double standard. Officer Charlie is still Charlie—clever, clumsy, graceful, good-hearted. In one scene he catches a woman stealing a ham, but her tears so move him that instead of arresting her, he steals some vegetables from a nearby grocer to make sure her dinner is well balanced. He is still Charlie, but now, working behind a policeman's badge, all his mischief is considered respectable. Even dreaded narcotics are turned to virtuous use in Charlie's veins. Society will accept in its own name what it condemns in outsiders.

The contradiction between society's stated aims and its reality is expressed at the beginning of *The Immigrant*, a film that millions in the United States at this time—immigrants themselves—

could appreciate. Charlie and Edna are immigrants on board a ship taking them from Europe to the New World. Like all the other passengers they are excited by the sight of the Statue of Liberty, gatepost to the United States. "The arrival in the Land of Liberty," proclaims the title on screen—and immediately the immigrants are herded together sardine-tight behind a rope barrier. Charlie takes a wry second glance at Miss Liberty. He gets the message: Welcome, immigrants, to the land of freedom and opportunity; welcome, cattle, to the slaughter.

Although social themes became stronger in Chaplin's four Mutual films in 1917, these two-reelers remained mainly "gag" films—that is, movies whose themes provided a core around which bits of funny business could be built. When he began his series for First National Pictures, however, Chaplin enlarged both his themes and his scale. Having built his own Hollywood studio, he was now ready to move from the fine drawings of the Essanay-Mutual period to the larger canvasses that would become his first full-fledged works of art.

The first thing that distinguished the First National releases from their predecessors was their length: *A Dog's Life* and *Shoulder Arms*, the first two movies made under the new contract, were each three reels long—roughly three-quarters of an hour. Never before had Chaplin intentionally made a film of more than two reels. Then there were other differences: more poetic, more substantial, and sometimes more biting themes; less slapstick than in any previous films.

In *A Dog's Life* the Tramp has something he has never had before: a real comrade. In the past the Tramp has had an occasional friend or business or drinking partner, but never a genuine comrade and colleague and constant companion like Scraps, the mutt which the Tramp has saved from attack by other dogs. In Scraps, the Tramp has a buddy at last. They are inseparable; their fortunes are linked to each other's; they are both for one and one for both. It is Charlie and Scraps all the way, down the line. Together they hunt for food and shelter, woo the lovely Edna, find some buried stolen money, lose it to crooks, capture the crooks, regain the money, rewoo the lovely Edna. In this film Charlie and

Edna wind up married and settle down on the farm he dreamed of in *The Tramp*. At its conclusion the happy couple gaze fondly into a cradle. The cradle holds Scraps and her puppies.

Although it stands on its own as a very funny movie, *A Dog's Life* is important in the history of Chaplin's movies for two reasons. First, it contains the element of partnership that Chaplin will return to in two of his later masterpieces. Scraps is really an extension of the Tramp; he is the dog that Charlie would be if Charlie were a dog. And a second reason for its uniqueness is its use of irony, the saying of one thing while intending another, opposite meaning. The gloom in the beginning scenes of *A Dog's Life* is so deep that the happiness that follows seems unrealistic, impossible. When we first meet Edna in this movie, she is so down in the dumps that she seems ready for suicide. The Tramp tries, but there is no way he can cheer her up. Then he produces a little money, and all is well: she is as happy as can be. But the viewer must know better than that: life's deepest problems are not cured so easily. In this film Chaplin, with uncharacteristic bitterness, seems to be saying: Sure, go ahead, believe it; if you want to think that a dog's friendship and a few dollars cash can right all wrongs, help yourself. To the realistic viewer, however, the easy happiness of *A Dog's Life* serves to heighten the more convincing bleakness.

World War I was still raging when *A Dog's Life* came out in 1918, and by then Charlie had become the most familiar human figure in the world. Many journalists called him that; no one disputed it. The most familiar human figure in the world cannot be a private person—not even if he shares a body with Charles Spencer Chaplin, a very private person indeed. And so, after he got the bitterness of *A Dog's Life* out of his system, Chaplin went to work on a movie—a very funny movie—about, of all things, that dirty, stinking war. The executives at First National all worried about it. Some of Chaplin's friends thought he was crazy. That horrible cancer that had already eaten up half the map of Europe—was that to be a laughing matter? Yes. He called it *Shoulder Arms*.

Charlie has been drafted, and after his first stop in a training camp, where he is easily the most inept buffoon in the ranks of buffoons, we find him in the trenches of France. A volunteer is needed to run a mission behind enemy German lines. Charlie will be the hero! To avoid detection he slips into an ingenious disguise, a tree trunk. Unfortunately for the little fellow, the German soldiers are then looking for firewood, and one by one they approach him to cut him down. Charlie outsmarts them, though, and by swinging his limbs around, knocks each enemy soldier out as he draws near. Eventually Charlie seeks shelter in a farm cottage and discovers Edna. For the fourteenth or fifteenth time on film, Charlie falls in love with her at first sight. The Germans arrive. Charlie escapes, but Edna is arrested. Craftily, Charlie goes to the German headquarters to rescue her, knocks out a German officer, and slips into his uniform. Then who should arrive but the German ruler himself, the Kaiser, who assumes that Charlie in his German uniform is his chauffeur. Charlie allows the Kaiser his misconception. He frees Edna and a captive Allied sergeant but remains to drive the Kaiser and Germany's two other most important leaders in their staff car. They tell driver Charlie where to take them but, while the three discuss the war, Charlie taxis Germany's high command right up into Allied headquarters. Charlie has single-handedly won the war! His buddies gather round, patting him on the back. But wait! Only one man is patting him on the back. Wake up, the man says. Charlie awakens. He is still in the training camp barracks. He has not yet even left the United States. Once again, it has all been a dream.

Shoulder Arms is a masterpiece. All the ingredients that made Charlie unique are present: the wonderful acting and pantomime, the graceful choreography, the perfect bits of business, and all the intangible qualities—pathos, irony, satire, and the blend of realism and fantasy. Not only are they all present; they are present in flawless proportion. Never before had the little Tramp seemed so human, so believable. The movie is a symphony of great movements and moments. Indeed, it is one of those few movies, most viewers agree, that you wish would go on and on. Moreover, many critics at the time believed that *Shoulder Arms* gave a better and more realistic picture of World War I than any documentary or dramatic film about the conflict. As the French artist-poet Jean Cocteau put it, "It moves like a drumroll."

Not surprisingly, *Shoulder Arms* is a portrait of the little guy, the ordinary soldier at war. It does not present the war in terms of an epic struggle or grand crusade. It tells of war from the point of view of the man in the trench, the citizen called to arms, who sees the war as filth and loneliness and danger and indignity. It captures this point of view perfectly—and yet, it never for an instant stops being a comedy.

Charlie's personality lights up *Shoulder Arms*, and though there is plenty of pathos, the overall tone is one of great optimism. If the little Tramp can keep his gentle nature and good humor through the carnage of this war, then humanity has not been crushed. The film is so rich in warm, priceless moments that no summary can do it justice. There is the pathetic scene in the trench when all the men are given packages from home. Charlie receives none. As the other soldiers unwrap their sausages and cheese, Charlie finds a mousetrap and begins to nibble at the little wedge of cheese. The others see him and sympathize; they offer to share their packages with him. No, no, Charlie gestures, this is fine, fine, my favorite kind, really. Charlie gets no letter, and so he steals up behind his buddies as they read theirs. As he reads over their shoulders, his face registers the right response to each letter. To interpret these responses the viewer needs no titles. When he reads a letter from a soldier's girl, Charlie's head tilts, he smiles sadly, he sighs with love and longing. When he reads a letter from a soldier's wife about their little child, Charlie's face beams with pride. A letter from a soldier's mom melts his face to tenderness and brings a tear to his eye; a footnote from dad stiffens his upper lip. It is an incredible performance, Chaplin at his most ingenious. Even the printed titles, which are used very sparingly, are splendid. When Charlie returns to headquarters alone with thirteen German prisoners, his comrades are flabbergasted. How did you, one man, capture thirteen enemy soldiers? they want to know. With a little shrug Charlie explains simply, "I surrounded them."

When prints of *Shoulder Arms* reached France, the armistice had already been declared, but the troops were still in the trenches. The movie was shown to them there. Some people worried. How would the soldiers feel seeing this terribly funny film about the bloody war they'd just been through? The sound from the trenches revealed what the soldiers thought. After every showing of *Shoulder Arms* the trenches came alive with the joyous shouts of Bravo Charlie; Bravo *Charlot*!

9

Charlie and the Kid

Shoulder Arms was a tough act to follow, and for a time Chaplin didn't try. He returned to two-reelers for his next pair of movies. *Sunnyside*, one of his most poetic films, contains a long dream sequence which is almost a ballet, and a nice, simple message. In this movie the Tramp, in an uncharacteristic move for him, tries to impress Edna by discarding his Tramp's getup in favor of a city slicker's clothing. All he manages to accomplish in his phoney guise is to make a fool of himself. The little message: be yourself.

A Day's Pleasure is unusual because Charlie is married and has a family in it—and even a Ford automobile—but for the most part this movie returns to the simpler Essanay-Mutual mold. One very funny scene begins with Charlie trying to set up a folding deck chair. We know what's coming; we know the relationship that exists between Charlie and inanimate objects. But our knowing doesn't make what's coming any the less funny.

One of Charlie and Edna's two sons in *A Day's Pleasure* was played by a youngster named Jackie Coogan. Chaplin had seen the boy for the first time on the vaudeville stage. The boy was four years old, and his father, a song-and-dance man, had brought Jackie onstage at the conclusion of his own performance to share a few bows. With just a wink and a wave and a couple of quick dance steps, Jackie captured the affection of the whole audience. Chaplin had been impressed and amused: the little boy seemed to radiate charm and personality. The memory of Jackie Coogan stuck with him; an idea began to take shape in his mind.

In 1919 Chaplin sent for Jackie's father and asked to use the boy in a movie. "All he has to do is make this one picture," Chaplin explained. "This story will give your son the opportunity of his life." Coogan agreed.

A Day's Pleasure was not the "one picture" that Chaplin meant. *A Day's Pleasure* was merely a dry run, Jackie's introduction to movie acting. After it was in the can, Chaplin and his discovery went to work on the big one.

The big one would be *The Kid*, a feature-length motion picture, six reels long. From the day the idea for the film came to him, Chaplin was driven by it; never before was he so much the perfectionist. More than ever he insisted that his players perform a scene over and over again until it was absolutely right—then he had them do it again so that it could be photographed from a different angle. At other times players would arrive at the studio and not work at all. Chaplin wanted every moment to be perfect; often he had to wait for an idea to come to him. And while he waited, the cast waited—for hours, sometimes days. Moreover, he was tense and touchy during filming. If a member of the company wanted to make a suggestion, he had to be careful to make it in a way that made Chaplin think it was *his* idea.

The main reason why Chaplin was so tense was the fact that he knew he was taking a terrific chance. *The Kid* was something new, a departure from his tried and true formula. His intuition had always guided him correctly before, but that was no consolation: the law of averages said that he would have to fail sometime. And if *The Kid* turned out to be that failure, it would be a colossal one.

One worry was the length of time he was taking to make the movie. The public, it was said, was fickle. Since 1914 the enthusiasm of his fans had been fed by a constant flow of new films. But *The Kid* took fifteen months to film; when 1920 came and went without a new Charlie adventure, public enthusiasm might cool down.

Another worry was the length of the movie. Comedies conventionally were short. The rare exception—such as Mack Sennett's

Tillie's Punctured Romance—succeeded with an all-star comedy cast and a plot jam-packed with fast-paced action. *The Kid* wasn't like that. It had no more players or gags than an average two-reeler, and its pacing was leisurely, more like the pacing of a drama than a traditional comedy.

Then there was the matter of content. "A picture with a smile and perhaps a tear," says the opening title of *The Kid*. How would a world of Charlie fans respond to a motion picture that mixed sadness with comedy, that might make them cry as well as laugh? Several of Chaplin's friends advised against the mixture. As the writer Gouverneur Morris put it to him, "The form must be pure, either slapstick or drama; you cannot mix them, otherwise one element of your story will fail." Were Morris and the others right?

The executives at First National did nothing to alleviate Chaplin's concern. Indeed, they had every right to be worried themselves. They had contracted for eight two-reelers. Two of the first four films Chaplin had turned out for them had been three-reelers. Well, that was all right: one extra reel added only ten or fifteen minutes to the usual length, and besides, those three-reelers had been enormously successful. But six reels—an hour and a half! Certainly it was possible that *The Kid* would make a fortune, but First National had not paid over a million dollars for possibilities; it had paid for sure things, and sure things were short.

Still, worried though he was, Chaplin knew that he had to make *The Kid*. The character he had created was artistically as well as literally splitting his seams. The Charlie of *A Dog's Life* and *Shoulder Arms* had gone about as far as he could go. He was a perfection now, and like a superbly cut jewel he needed the proper setting to display all of his facets, his depths, and his brilliance.

But was *The Kid* that worthy setting? Chaplin wondered about that. By the time the studio work was done, the cast and crew were exhausted. When they saw the rough prints of the film, their response was listless. As Chaplin recalled it, "Nothing looked as funny or as interesting as we had imagined."

Worries notwithstanding, *The Kid* had to be put to the test. In those days—and the practice has continued to this day—moviemakers tested their films at a preview; most often they used the "sneak" preview, which audiences loved. The director and sometimes other studio chiefs attended the preview, and if the audience laughed when the film was supposed to be funny or gasped when its suspense built, then the film was ready to be released. If not, more work had to be done.

Chaplin took *The Kid* to Salt Lake City, Utah, to preview it. He was in a worrying mood that day. The big theater was about three-quarters full, and the audience didn't seem to like the regular feature. He worried that the patrons would apply their bad humor to his film. When the words "Charlie Chaplin in" hit the screen, however, the surprised patrons cried out in delight. Now *that* worried him: perhaps their expectations were too high and they would be disappointed. Then he worried throughout the first half-reel: the audience was so quiet. No matter that he had intended it that way, that the first seven or eight minutes were meant to be slow and solemn. As soon as the Tramp appeared, though, the moviegoers laughed. Before he'd even done anything funny, they laughed. Chaplin started to relax a little. Perhaps it was then that he realized the power of the little fellow on the screen. For the Tramp was so familiar, so much an institution, that his mere appearance stimulated laughter—a laughter of memory as much as action, a laughter accumulated in six years and through nearly seventy movies. By the time the sneak preview of *The Kid* was over, Chaplin knew he had a hit.

The first person we meet in *The Kid* is Edna, the downcast, world-weary Edna we met early in *A Dog's Life*. Poor, jobless, unmarried, she is afraid that she won't be able to care for her newborn baby, which she carries in her arms. She notices a splendid new limousine parked at the curb. Surely the owner of such a fine car must be very rich—rich enough to raise a child properly. She writes a note asking the owner to care for her son and puts the baby on the back seat. While Jackie sleeps, thieves steal the car. When they notice the bundle in back, they dump it in an alley. Meanwhile Edna changes her mind. She races back, but the car is gone. While she grieves, her son lies sleeping in the slums.

Out for a jaunty walk, his cane swinging happily to bat away garbage thrown from windows, Charlie comes across the bundle of life. At first he is not enchanted. An old lady comes by pushing a baby buggy, and Charlie tries to slip the infant into the buggy. The lady will have none of it. A moment later he passes an open manhole. He looks at the bundle in his arms, then down the hole. Should he? It would be so easy. But no, of course not. He takes the baby home to his horrible cellar flat, finds the mother's note, and decides to raise the boy himself.

Five years pass. The baby has become the Kid. The Kid is played by Jackie Coogan. This role will make Jackie the screen's first celebrated child star.

Charlie and the Kid are father and son, and they are more: they are friends and partners. And even more than that, they are mirror reflections of each other separated by time. As Charlie manicures his nails before dining, so does Jackie. What the Tramp laughs and frowns at, the Kid laughs and frowns at. The Kid is a junior version of the Tramp, the Tramp a senior version of the Kid.

They are a hardworking pair. Charlie is a window mender. The Kid's job is to throw rocks through windows. Moments after the glass breaks, Charlie knocks on the door and offers to repair the broken pane. In one famous scene the Kid is about to hurl a rock, but when he brings his arm back to let loose, his hand touches the coat of a policeman. The Kid glances back and, without a second's hesitation, smiles, tosses the rock straight up in the air a few feet, catches it, and continues his game of catch as he slowly strolls, then suddenly sprints off down the street. His reaction is precisely what Charlie's would have been.

We have never seen Charlie so happy. He is an attentive father, a constant teacher, but as good a listener as he is a lecturer. His every mannerism and expression broadcasts his love for the Kid, and Jackie obviously adores Charlie. For the first time in his life Charlie is not lonely. And the Kid—well, the Kid is lucky. He is lucky that he is not being raised by the owner of the swell limousine. No child ever had a happier, richer life than the Kid.

In one way life has been kind to Edna, too: she has become a successful singer. But, lonely and feeling guilty for having abandoned her son, she befriends the children of the slums. She even knows the Kid, but she does not know that he is hers. One day she stops a fight. The Kid is hurt, and Edna tells Charlie to take him to a doctor.

Charlie has always insisted that the Kid should wear his mother's note inside his shirt. When the doctor examines the boy he finds the note. Learning that Charlie is not the Kid's legal father, the doctor notifies the authorities, the Child Welfare Service.

The authorities represent society. Society has its rule book. It says: Here is a little boy living in a basement flat with a man who is not legally his father; we must take the boy away and make him respectable. Do the authorities look at the facts? Do they even look at the Kid? No. If they did, they would see a healthy and high-spirited youngster, full of life, loving and loved, with wonderful manners and joy in his eyes. He couldn't have gotten that way on his own. He must have had proper—no, expert—guidance. But the authorities aren't interested. They operate by rules, by technicalities, not by truths.

So the authorities take the Kid away in a truck, but Charlie slips into the truck and lets the Kid out. They hide for the night in a rooming house.

Meanwhile the doctor tells Edna about the note he found on the Kid, and of course Edna realizes it is her own. She places an advertisement in the newspaper, offering a reward for the return of her son. The man who runs the rooming house recognizes the description, steals the Kid, and returns him to his mother.

Charlie's movements when he realizes the Kid is gone say everything. "Jack! Jack!" he cries, and every step, every disappointed glance is tortured, tormented, unbearably sad. It is as if his life's blood is draining away; certainly his reason for living is gone. Finally, in total exhaustion and despair, he slumps down to the ground and sleeps. He sleeps and he dreams . . .

He dreams of Heaven. His Heaven is the same slum street

of the film, and the London slum street of Chaplin's youth. The angels have white wings attached to their same ratty slum clothing. The houses are still ramshackle, but they are decorated with garlands of flowers. The residents still quarrel; their arguments are still quelled by a policeman. But Heaven it surely is . . .

Just as Heaven it had been for seven-year-old Charles Chaplin in London in the mid 1890s. The street was a slum, and the smells were atrocious, but it was Heaven because Hannah Chaplin was home, and the workhouse was behind them, and Hannah and Charlie and Sydney were together again. And that's all that Heaven could be—a place where people who loved each other were together. . . .

And the slum street Chaplin creates for Charlie's dream is Heaven because Charlie and the Kid are there together. For five years Charlie, poor as ever, bedraggled as ever, had in fact been living in a Heaven on earth. He loved the Kid, and the Kid loved him; they were together, and there could be no better world than that; it was perfection, Heaven. Now it is gone. Now it is only a dream world. "Jack! Jack!" Charlie's anguished cries seem to echo through the silent dream in a mute drama. Hold on, Charlie, hold on to the Kid and to the Heaven you held in your hands; and he tries to hold on, but a dream won't be held, and it slips, fades, dies . . .

Hey, bub, wake up, wake up: a policeman shakes him, rouses him from sleep, takes him away from the Kid and Heaven. Come with me, the cop says. Charlie follows. The cop takes him to a fine house, knocks on the door, leaves him there. The big door opens. Behind it are Edna and the Kid, welcoming Charlie home.

10

Real and True to Life

When the men of First National Pictures found out about the length of *The Kid*, they told Chaplin that they planned to break it up and release it as three separate two-reelers. If Chaplin had been Charlie, he undoubtedly would have responded with a thumb of the nose and a quick kick in the pants. But off-camera Chaplin never was Charlie, and so he simply replied that they would do no such thing; he would take them to court to stop them and very possibly make a mess of the films he still owed them under their contract. The First National executives wisely backed down.

Artistically, critically, financially, *The Kid* was an enormous success. Chaplin's intuition had been right again. The Tramp was now a fully rounded comic and dramatic character. Once again he needed a larger setting in which to flourish. He needed motion pictures of feature length.

But making long movies in association with First National was out of the question. Chaplin needed complete freedom, and that included the freedom to take his time. The pressure exerted on him by the First National executives reduced that freedom. And the mentality that would even suggest breaking up a masterpiece like *The Kid* was unspeakable.

Chaplin was not the only artist in Hollywood who resented the men at the distribution end of the motion-picture industry. In 1919, in order to free themselves from the businessmen's influence, Chaplin and several other independent producers formed their own distributing company. His partners were Douglas Fairbanks, the dashing and popular hero of countless costume-adventure films; Mary Pickford, "America's Sweetheart" (and later Fairbanks' wife); D. W. Griffith, the world's most widely admired director at the time; and the popular cowboy star William S. Hart. Without question the greatest names in movies in that period, these film-makers were able, because of their company, to maintain their independence. And for more than thirty years the name of their distributing company, United Artists, at the beginning of a movie was the most respected in the business and a symbol of quality.

But before he could begin distributing his movies through United Artists, Chaplin had to fulfill his contract with First National Pictures. After *The Kid*, he made two two-reelers, *The Idle Class* and *Pay Day*, and a four-reeler, *The Pilgrim*. Thereafter he was on his own, and thereafter he made only feature-length films.

The Idle Class is about manners. In many of his films, Charlie demonstrates that he knows that society likes things done in certain ways. What Charlie does not understand is that misplaced manners are ridiculous. His ignorance of this fact is what makes him so funny. Before dining he meticulously manicures his fingernails, and afterward he cleans up with a fingerbowl. Good manners in a grand dining room, these gestures seem ridiculous when done by a vagabond seated beside a dusty road about to eat a handout and when the fingerbowl is a tomato can. When completing a meal in a restaurant with Edna and a new friend, Charlie insists on paying the check. No, no, I insist, says the other man; No, no, but *I* insist, gestures Charlie; and back and forth they insist, taking the check from one another with all the grandness of two wealthy gentlemen. Finally the friend gives in, and now Charlie's gentlemanliness is ridiculous because of course he has no money. When Charlie wants to smoke, he removes a cigarette from a shiny cigarette case with the nonchalance of an aristocrat—only the cigarette case is a polished sardine can and the cigarette a tiny butt. When Charlie removes his gloves, he does so with letter-perfect finesse—daintily, a finger at a time—

only the fingers come off, leaving a ratty mitten on the palm of his hand. Done by Charlie, these perfect demonstrations of perfect manners are absurd.

The Idle Class contrasts the lives of the Tramp and a rich gentleman, also played by Chaplin. Even before they are aware of one another's existence, the rich and poor look-alikes are living the same sort of lives. Both travel south in the wintertime; both are golfers; both enjoy a masquerade ball. Needless to say, the similarities do not go very deep. The millionaire Charlie travels in comfort while the Tramp hops a ride on a freight or an auto bumper. The rich man lives in the finest hotel suite while the poor Charlie sleeps wherever he won't get caught and thrown out. Their *form*, however, is identical—the Tramp swings his golf club with absolute perfection, and his manners, as always, are impeccable. Indeed, he looks so much the gentleman that when he wanders into a masquerade party, the rich Charlie's wife, Edna, thinks he is her husband dressed in the costume of a tramp. She is so delighted that he is sober for a change that she becomes very affectionate. When the real husband—clothed in knight's armor and drunk to his helmet—arrives, Edna realizes that she's made a fool of herself. Humiliated, she sends the little fellow away. A moment later she feels guilty. Was the affair the Tramp's fault? No. If her no-good husband had been sober and on time, there would have been no misunderstanding. She sends her father after the Tramp. Tell the little fellow we are sorry, she instructs him; tell him that we care for him and want to help him and be his friend. The father catches up to Charlie and delivers the message. Charlie points to the ground. His gesture says, Hey, look at that, way down there! The man bends way over to see—and a quick kick in the pants lays him flat on the ground. That's what Charlie thinks of the help and friendship of the rich.

All is form, Chaplin says in *The Idle Class*. In all their interests and activities the rich and poor Charlies are the same. The poor Charlie is actually a better man than the rich: he even sees the good in Edna, whereas her husband sees only the nagging wife. The rich Charlie is more acceptable to society, however, because he is rich.

In 1921, when Chaplin made *The Idle Class*, the United States was early along in that fantastic period known as the Roaring Twenties. Although it is remembered as a prosperous era, its riches were not evenly or even proportionately distributed. The stock market was soaring, but so was the rate of unemployment. The rich were getting richer; the middle classes were prospering, too, but the poor were staying poor. The chasm between the poor and the others was growing wider. As often happens when people become rich quickly in boom times, those with money often thought that they were better than the poor because they were richer than the poor. *The Idle Class* contradicts that notion. The rich are richer than the poor for one reason and one reason only, the movie says: because they have more money.

Charlie is an outsider; he does not march to the beat of society's drum. He is too concerned with his own survival to worry about society's laws: if he must steal food to avoid starving, he will steal. He is too concerned with preserving his own dignity to worry about society's judgment: if society wishes to call him ridiculous for polishing his fingernails before dining on scraps, that is society's problem. Being a homeless tramp doesn't mean that he must live without elegance. But though he undoubtedly is out of step with conventional society, Charlie does live his life according to law—moral law. And so in the end Charlie is really quite a good citizen because, given a choice between right and wrong, he always chooses right.

In *The Pilgrim* Charlie is the classic example of society's outsider—an escaped convict. In order to conceal his identity, he steals the clothes of a parson as that gentleman bathes in a lake. The parson's garments, like the uniform and badge in *Easy Street*, convert Charlie from a social outcast to a respectable member of society. He hops a train, and when he gets off in a small town in the Southwest, he is greeted by a welcoming committee. It seems that the townspeople have been expecting their new parson and assume Charlie is he. They are so excited that they ask him to conduct a church service right away. One of Chaplin's great demonstrations of mime, the sermon in church tells the story, with gesture and dance, of David and Goliath. Charlie really gets carried away by this performance; he makes the Hebrew boy and the Philistine giant come alive. But he does not tell the story the traditional way; in his version they are not so much enemies as a pair of noble gladiators or prizefighters who respect one another. Goliath must fall because youth and cunning and poetry must always triumph over age and primitive strength, but he falls with honor.

Charlie the "parson" is invited to have Sunday dinner with Edna and her mother. Through their small-town home that afternoon passes a typical succession of do-gooding hypocrites. The town elders are fat, self-satisfied businessmen, pious and pompous, who evidently think that the presence of a parson makes their town respectable. A little boy visits, and as all the grown-ups dote on him, he slyly throws goldfish into the flowers and slaps flypaper onto the seats of ladies' dresses. Parson Charlie speaks affectionately to the evil little creature until no one else is present. Then he gracefully delivers one swift kick to the middle of the child's little belly.

Charlie does not mind his pose, for everyone, it seems, is living some sort of pose in this hypocritical little town (everyone except the pure and innocent Edna). But later he is faced with a moral dilemma. A crook arrives and steals Edna's mortgage money. Charlie knows the crook from prison. He can't expose the criminal, for if he does, the man will expose him; but he can't let the thief steal the money, either.

Charlie finally does recapture the money. When he returns it to Edna, he is exposed. Now the sheriff is after him. Edna tries to intervene, but the sheriff chases Charlie south. Catching him near the Mexican-American border, the sheriff decides to give Charlie a break. The sheriff tells Charlie to go pick some flowers growing on the Mexican side of the border. He is really telling Charlie to cross the border to the flowers, where he will be a free man. Charlie goes into Mexico to get the flowers, but he is extremely moved by the sheriff's generosity. Characteristically, Charlie must give the sheriff a token of his gratitude. So he recrosses the border and presents the bouquet to the lawman. Oh, good heavens! says the sheriff's exasperated expression, and to make his point more strongly, he boots the Tramp back into Mexico and rides away. From deeper in Mexico comes a gang of bandits, pistols firing. What to do! In one country are freedom and flowers but bandits; in the other are prison and the crook's revenge. Neither choice seems very good. The bandits ride closer; Charlie, one foot in the United States, one foot in Mexico, skips, then runs. He is still running, still straddling the border, as *The Pilgrim* ends.

"Comedy must be real and true to life," Chaplin told reporters when asked to define the secret of his formula. *The Idle Class* and *The Pilgrim*, even more than the more poetic *The Kid*, illustrate this notion. *The Pilgrim* rings particularly true. There is almost nothing fanciful about it. In it society's outcast becomes respectable because of a costume. But moral law—not social law—forces Charlie to reveal himself. He learns that life is a balancing act, that few important decisions are easy, that images are tricky. The piety of leadership is a cover-up for corruption. An adorable child is a devil. The only trustworthy quality is innocence. Only the innocent have the power to look beyond society's conventions and see the truth. Edna is innocent. Good old Edna. Only Edna knows that the convict dressed as a parson has the purest heart in town. Only Edna knows how good a citizen Charlie really is.

11

The Chaplin Touch

Chaplin had every reason to be happy. He was rich and famous and loved the world around. He was on his own now, his own boss, able to work at his own pace, free of the meddling and pressures of distributors. But he wasn't happy because he was lonely. He had no comfortable place to rest himself, no real home.

He had had an empty marriage that had failed. The failure not only cost him a wife; it spoiled the very special relationship he had had with Edna Purviance. In a way, that was the greater loss, for Edna had been the only constant woman companion he had ever had.

After the war he and Sydney had brought their mother to the United States. They employed nurses and companions and gave her a life of luxury in a lovely house by the sea. But Hannah Chaplin was not well. She had long blank spells when she understood nothing. She never did comprehend that her son was the most familiar human figure in the world—or even that he was a great success. She enjoyed it when he showed her his films, but there is some doubt whether she recognized the figure on the screen as her son. He visited her often, but his visits depressed him and left him feeling emptier and more alone than ever.

After completing *The Idle Class* in 1921, Chaplin suddenly shut down the studio and took a trip abroad. He simply had to get away from California. It was a fine idea, and for a time it restored his spirits. He returned to England like a conquering hero. Mobs enveloped him at the dock and at every train station.

He recalled his roots and realized how far he had come: by day he revisited the shabby slums of his childhood, and in the evening he dined with England's most distinguished aristocrats. Then he went to Paris, where he was received with equal fervor. He was delighted by his reception there. Whenever French people asked for his autograph, he proudly signed "Charlot" with grand flourishes. Finally, he had a quieter stay in Berlin. (Because of the war and its troubled aftermath, his films had not yet been shown in Germany.)

When he returned home, Chaplin was so excited that, on the westbound train, he began writing an account of his tour. He started it in New York, and by the time he reached Utah, he had written a whole book, *My Wonderful Visit*. Back in California, he called on the movie producer Samuel Goldwyn and kept his host up half the night as he described and acted out every adventure he had had abroad.

But the emptiness soon returned. He buried himself in his work. His passion for perfection was a reflection of his loneliness. Since his work was all he had, he gave himself to it body and soul.

Chaplin's first feature for United Artists was not a Charlie Chaplin comedy. It was a drama called *A Woman of Paris*, and except for a brief appearance as a railroad porter, Chaplin wasn't even in it. He was its writer and director, however, and it was one of the most important movies of the 1920s.

There were two main reasons why Chaplin made *A Woman of Paris*. One was Edna Purviance. Edna had outgrown the sweet and innocent girlishness that had made her an ideal leading lady for the Tramp. She was twenty-six in 1922, the year when *The Pilgrim* was shot, a mature, handsome, full-figured woman who looked better suited to elegant gowns and surroundings than to the homely settings of Charlie's world. Both Chaplin and Edna knew that they were approaching the end of their onscreen partnership, and Chaplin wanted to help her start a new career as a dramatic actress. *A Woman of Paris* was his way of helping.

The other reason why Chaplin wanted to make *A Woman of Paris* was artistic. After eight years in the movie business, Chaplin had formed some pretty strong opinions about the art of the cinema. His fellow artists and all the world had applauded his art, and everyone in the know understood how influential his work had been. But most people associated his accomplishments with comedy. Chaplin was anxious to demonstrate that his approach and techniques applied to all movies, not just to comedy. *A Woman of Paris* became that demonstration.

Chaplin's approach to film-making had always been influential. One of the movies' most exacting artists, he shot thousands of feet of film to get hundreds. He filmed scenes over and over again until they were right. Often he shot a sequence, showed it to a colleague or studio visitor, and asked the viewer to explain what he'd just seen. If the explanation wasn't crystal clear or if any part of the scene was unnoticed or misunderstood, he shot it again. And again. And again—until it was correct.

He believed in simplicity. He tried to advance the story with visual devices rather than with printed explanations. In himself and in the players whom he directed, he strove to simplify poses, gestures, movements to make them descriptive. The way Charlie read his buddies' letters over their shoulders in *Shoulder Arms* was a good example of this simplicity. The Tramp's expressions revealed the contents of the letters and reminded us that he was lonely and had no one waiting for him at home. They also told us that the other soldiers missed their homes and families. In a few moments Chaplin conveyed the message that the war was being fought by ordinary men who would rather be home. To achieve such perfect simplicity required a lot of work.

Because of the commercial success of Chaplin's films, artistry in film-making became respectable. The movies of the other great early cinema artist, D. W. Griffith, had not consistently been making money. Without Chaplin to prove that quality paid, the businessmen who ran the movies might have completely overpowered the artists. The businessmen's budgets were indeed powerful influences on the film-makers, but so was Chaplin's example to make a film right. His influence was substantially responsible for making the Hollywood movie the most handsomely crafted in the world.

But Chaplin's greatest influence was on film acting—his own

and the acting of those he directed. During the first eight years of his career, this influence colored only film comedy. Chaplin felt, however, that his sort of acting was appropriate for all movies.

From the earliest days of the art, film-makers knew that traditional stage acting did not work in movies. For in silent films, the traditional actor's most expressive tool, his voice, was useless. In a stage play a woman threatened by a cruel villain might cry out, "No! No! Don't hurt me! Don't come any closer!" and the audience would of course know that she was in trouble and frightened. In a silent photoplay the voiceless actress would have to express herself some other way. One way was with printed titles on the screen. But printed messages did not really express emotion, and besides, printed words interrupted the flow of the drama and were always kept to an absolute minimum. Another way was with pantomime. In a silent melodrama a woman threatened by a cruel oncoming villain would express her response with broad gesture and expression. She would lean backward, her torso turned away from the villain, put her opened hands up in front of her at shoulder level, turn her mouth down in sorrow, and open her eyes wide in fright. Her pose would express her fear.

To early film-makers, big, broad pantomime seemed a logical acting substitution for the voice. The only thing wrong with that logic was that it neglected the main new tool of a brand-new art: the camera. For if it was true that film took away the actor's voice, it was also true that the camera moved in close and gave the actor the use of his face.

Except for the broadest sort of expressions, the face had never been available to stage actors as an instrument of expressing emotion. The motion-picture camera made this instrument available. The human face is a marvelously expressive surface: the slightest turn of mouth, lift of eyebrow, thrust of chin can convey the deepest meaning. The motion-picture camera can actually examine a face more closely than most people ever get a chance to. Except in extraordinary circumstances, we do not look long and blatantly into the face of the person to whom we are talking; if we did, the person might feel self-conscious and look away or make a point of keeping emotion off his face. The camera can linger for a long time on an actor's face—it *wants* to convey emotion—and the projector enlarges that face to a size bigger than life. The camera thus creates an intimacy between the player and his audience. This intimacy was the real compensation, in silent movies, for the absence of voices. And it was this intimacy that made the broad pantomime of early movies seem posed and false. After all, when photographed by the intimate camera, the actress's contorted posture and exaggerated expressions were blown up larger than life, too. While trying to make up for the lack of sound, she actually added another unreal touch.

Chaplin's intuition told him that broad pantomime was inappropriate for movies, and in his very first film for Keystone, *Making a Living*, he had demonstrated how correct his intuition was. There is a moment early in that picture when the Chaplin character borrows some money from an acquaintance. As the man reaches down into his pocket to get the money, Chaplin almost imperceptibly shifts his weight from one foot to the other, frowns just a little, and scratches his cheek. The sequence of gestures is very quick, very slight, and very simple, but it conveys in that moment the embarrassment that anyone might feel just after he's asked for a loan.

Chaplin's intuition was backed by his experience as an English music-hall performer. The English tradition of the deadpan clown was based on the idea that *no* expression is sometimes the *most* expressive look. A thousand horrible things might happen to an English clown, but he kept his face a blank. This was funny, but it also made for good acting: the blankness said, in effect, that any one expression would be inadequate to describe the horror of what had just happened to him.

Chaplin was not a deadpan actor, but in contrast to the usual players in silent films, he underemphasized rather than exaggerated his facial expressions. His standard expression was one of pleasant innocence spiced with just a touch of mischief around the eyes. He was very stingy with more descriptive expressions. Against this general blankness, each real—and always simplified

—expression stood out sharply and conveyed the emotion beneath it in an instant. In his 1915 movie *The Champion*, Charlie sits down on a step with his dog Spike and takes a frankfurter out of his pocket. He is about to take a bite when he looks at the dog. He looks back, straight at the camera, no expression on his face. He doesn't need one; his looking at the camera and the fact that he hasn't taken the bite of the hot dog tell us that he is thinking; and in that same instant he holds the frankfurter out to Spike. What he was thinking, then, was that Spike is hungry, too. But Spike turns his nose away from the frank. Charlie looks at the dog again, heaves a sigh, reaches into his pocket, removes a salt shaker, salts the frankfurter, and, while looking straight into the camera once more and frowning ever so slightly with a corner of his mouth, presents the food to Spike. This time the dog accepts his share. Charlie's expressions are slight and swift, probably less intense than they would be if they were used to express corresponding emotions in real life. But because they are so sharply drawn against the blankness, they are immediately revealing. The first glance into the camera tells us that his pesty conscience won't let him eat the whole frankfurter while the dog goes hungry. The sigh shows that he realizes why the finicky dog won't take a bite. The slight frown says that he feels pretty silly sitting there after giving in to the dog's whim. All the dogs in the world, and I've got to team up with one who won't eat without salt: that is the whole effect of the very simple expression.

Chaplin's understated acting made a quick impression on other film comedians. The great comic acrobat Harold Lloyd and the baby-faced, always victimized Harry Langdon played it straight for the camera. Buster Keaton made a brilliant career as a comedian who displayed virtually no facial expressions; he was the ultimate deadpan. And in his own movies Chaplin directed his players to keep their acting simple and underexpressed. "Don't act!" he said over and over again, and "Don't sell it!" "Think the scene," he would say. "If you think the scene it will get over." One of his favorite instructions was, "Remember, they're peeking at you." "I don't care what you do with your hands and feet," he'd say; if the players would simply put themselves into the situations of the characters, the "peeking" audience would recognize the emotions. But at the heart was "Don't act! Don't sell it! Don't act! Don't act!"

Chaplin believed that those instructions should apply to all movie acting, not just to comedy. Essentially, those instructions characterized the difference between stage and screen acting. Onstage an actor had to project his character and emotions outward; in film-making the camera brought the audience inward. The actor didn't have to project; he simply had to "be."

In *A Woman of Paris* Chaplin brought his acting techniques to drama. Not only did he have his players execute the understated acting style, but he used the intimate camera to highlight details of background and atmosphere in a simpler and more descriptive way than had ever been done before. Moving lights on a wall indicate that a train is passing. A shot of a few roofs suggests a small French town. A corner and a lamppost indicate the kind of neighborhood. In one scene, the relationship between the two principal characters is defined in a single action: Pierre simply opens one of Marie's bureau drawers and removes one of his own handkerchiefs. The audience is therefore instantly told that Pierre and Marie are living together. In another scene Marie is getting a massage. She is never seen; only the masseuse's face and upper torso are shown, but the masseuse's slight expressions and shoulder movements clearly show what part of Marie's body she is massaging.

The impact of *A Woman of Paris* was instantaneous. The film scarcely broke even commercially, but critics and film-makers were amazed. It was as if everyone realized, at once, that Chaplin was right. Broad pantomime was suddenly all but obsolete. And Chaplin's understated style of movie acting has prevailed ever since.

The film influenced almost everybody, but one of the most important of its admirers was a director named Ernst Lubitsch. Lubitsch, famous for his lavish costume dramas in his native Germany, arrived in Hollywood in 1923, the year *A Woman of Paris* was released. When Lubitsch saw the film, he couldn't get over it. He said himself that the Chaplin picture was made the way movies should be made. He changed his whole style, adopting the understated acting and especially the simplicity of Chaplin's technique.

Lubitsch is often called the inventor of the Hollywood movie—the swiftly paced, well-constructed, technically superb sort of motion picture that Hollywood became famous for. After seeing *A Woman of Paris*, Lubitsch began to photograph simple objects to tell his story—an empty coatrack to show that all the guests had gone home or a closed bedroom door to show where two lovers had gone. This technique came to be called "the Lubitsch touch" and was imitated by many other directors. But it was the same technique that Chaplin had used with lampposts and the bureau drawer in *A Woman of Paris*. As Lubitsch often pointed out, the Lubitsch touch was really the Chaplin touch.

Unfortunately, *A Woman of Paris* did not achieve the first of its aims. Critical response to Edna Purviance's performance as an embittered, worldly woman was good, but the public couldn't accept her this way. Her sympathetic personality, her role as the Tramp's sweetheart, was too deeply embedded in the audience's mind. As a result of the public's rejection of the "new" Edna, other directors were reluctant to use her. After *A Woman of Paris*, Edna's career ground to a halt.

After she retired, Chaplin and Edna kept in touch. They may not have seen each other often, but their bond was strong. Edna's occasional notes to Chaplin were filled with friendship—and always ended with a horrendously silly joke. And in his autobiography, Chaplin evokes more warmth writing about Edna than about any other person except his brother Sydney and his last wife, Oona. Although tender feelings are not something usually measured in dollars and cents, Chaplin did express his affection in a financial way. Edna and Chaplin stopped working together in 1923. She died in 1958. Edna had remained on his payroll and received her salary every week of her life.

12

Life—From a Distance

After *A Woman of Paris*, Chaplin began to plan a movie based on the Klondike gold rush. At first he toyed with the idea of going to Alaska to shoot it, but the problems would have been much too great. Instead he found a rugged area in the Rocky Mountains and had the Klondike duplicated there, complete with tons and tons of fake snow.

Begun in 1924, *The Gold Rush* was to be the film that would introduce the public to Chaplin's new leading lady, Lita Grey. And Lita Grey was to be—or so Chaplin thought for a time—his new and permanent defense against loneliness. As things turned out, however, the experience with Lita Grey almost destroyed him.

Lita Grey was the screen name of Lolita MacMurray. At the age of twelve, in 1920, she had been one of the children in the dream sequence of *The Kid*. Her mother, Lillian MacMurray, was an occasional actress who was determined that Lita would have the glorious screen career that she had once dreamed of for herself. Lillian encouraged Lita to endear herself to Chaplin, which was easy: Lita was a gorgeous child with a gay manner and a captivating smile. Chaplin gave both mother and daughter small roles as Edna's maids in *The Idle Class*. Thereafter, Lillian and Lita were frequent presences at the studio. Lita filled out and developed into an extremely attractive young woman. Chaplin could never resist that sort of innocent beauty, and Lillian knew it. When Lita was fifteen, her mother virtually thrust her into

Chaplin's arms. And Lita was all the more appealing because she really was innocent. Chaplin signed Lita to a contract; she was to be his leading lady in *The Gold Rush*. Before long, Lita, now sixteen, was pregnant, and she and Chaplin married.

Chaplin desperately wanted a wife and family and would have worked to make the marriage a good one—he adored Lita's looks and was proud of her vitality—but he had not counted on Lillian MacMurray. She immediately tried to run their lives. Lillian turned the Chaplin home into a center of social activity, a constant ballroom. Crowds of drinking flappers and swells danced in and out, day and night. After a tough day at the studio, Chaplin, who always had lived quietly, could not face the noise and the partygoers. He took to driving his car alone, aimlessly, late into the night, or sleeping at the Athletic Club to avoid the fun. Moreover, Lita was not exactly radiant before the camera. The role did not demand deep interpretive acting, but it did require freshness, and how could Lita be fresh after nightly parties? Lillian tried to run the studio, too, for Lita's convenience, and that was a mistake. Where work was at issue, Chaplin was an absolute despot, his studio a realm where his rule was law. When Lillian tried to interfere with his direction, she found herself up against a stone wall. Chaplin fired Lita and hired Georgia Hale in her place; thousands of feet of expensive film had to be reshot. Lillian and Lita were banned from the studio. For that Lillian never forgave Chaplin. She increased the pace of social activities, spent small fortunes, made him feel like an intruder in his own house. He hardly ever went home anymore.

When *The Gold Rush* was finished, Chaplin tried to spend more time at home with Lita and their newborn son, Charles, Jr. He simply could not endure Lillian and her constant friends, however, and so—unusually fast for him in those slow-thinking, long-planning days—he started his next movie immediately. While he was shooting *The Circus*, Lita gave birth to their second son, Sydney, named, of course, after Chaplin's brother.

One evening Chaplin came home after a very hard day to find his house packed with especially noisy, especially rowdy guests. His temper snapped and he ordered the guests to leave. Lita and

"A picture with a smile and perhaps a tear": *The Kid*.

A great team: Charlie and Jackie Coogan in Chaplin's
first feature-length movie, *The Kid* (1921). Here
they try to avoid the threat to their happy existence, the cop.

In this shot from *The Pilgrim* (1923),
Charlie-the-parson mimes the tale of David and Goliath.

The most popular stars
of their day,
Charles Chaplin mimics
Mary Pickford, and
Mary and Douglas Fairbanks
stand like Charlie. In 1919 the
trio were among the founders
of United Artists, a movie
distribution company.

In Charlie's getup (above), Chaplin
checks camera angles during
the filming of *The Gold Rush*
(1925). This feature-
length picture has the
strongest story structure
of all Chaplin's films
up to this time. Charlie (at right)
as the lone prospector.

CHARLIE AT HIS PEAK *City Lights* (1931)
contains some of Chaplin's finest acting and funniest bits
of business; but it is unique mainly because Charlie's character changes in it—changes from within. In *City Lights*,
for the first time in his film life, Charlie is forced to see
himself as others see him. And seeing himself that way
must change his own vision of himself for all time.

Early in *City Lights* Charlie meets and falls in love with
the blind flower girl, played by Virginia Cherrill.

Charlie meets the millionaire (Harry Myers). When he is drunk, the millionaire is the Tramp's best buddy; when he sobers up, he hasn't the faintest idea who Charlie is.

In the locker room before the big prizefight, Charlie tries to charm his opponent. He appears to be failing.

Arrested by plainclothes cops on the street, Charlie
drops his cane. Suddenly the newsboys who have been
tormenting him throughout the film come to his aid.

Charlie at his most sublime and saddest:
the look of love and loss that brings *City Lights* to a close.

Lillian stormed out, too, taking the two little boys with them.

Lita sued for divorce, and her mother took her case to the newspapers. Chaplin was accused of unspeakable cruelty and inhuman crimes. The sensational stories blared from the daily headlines. As was his habit, Chaplin retreated into silence and work. He toiled like a slave on *The Circus*. Exhausted and depressed, unwilling to dignify the appalling accusations by answering them, he pushed himself to the brink of nervous collapse. To make matters worse, his mother had a stroke, lingered for a couple of days in a coma, and died. He was so despondent that some of his colleagues feared that he might commit suicide.

The final blow came when Lita's lawyers shut down his studio. Now he could not even lose himself in work. Chaplin fled to New York to see his lawyer. His lawyer took one look at him and called in a team of doctors. It was a wise move. Chaplin was in a state of emotional collapse. The doctors saved his sanity just when he was on the brink of losing it.

Chaplin paid Lita Grey a settlement of one million dollars for the divorce. His reputation ruined, his health fragile, he returned to Los Angeles and *The Circus*. Although his associates doubted that he was strong enough, he finished the movie with his usual professional thoroughness and care. *The Circus* contained many of his funniest bits of business, but, not surprisingly, it was his saddest film by far.

Chaplin had often said that he believed that comedy should be "real and true to life." Later—after his personal problems of the 1920s—he grew fond of saying that comedy should present a picture of "life—from a distance." The second statement in no way contradicts the first, but it does reveal that he had broadened his vision. His personal anguish, as he himself admitted, was responsible more than a little for his broader view. He felt more of the pain of life, and therefore he knew more of life, and he put all his new knowledge into his films. By "distance" he did not mean detachment. By distance he meant the kind a painter places between himself and a still life or street scene. The painter needs distance to see his subject whole. For Chaplin good comedy required a similar distance between life and the artist.

With *The Gold Rush* and *The Circus*, Chaplin had begun to step back from his subject, to see the whole of life, and to deal realistically and reasonably with the problems of life as he never had before. To his credit, he did not allow his personal problems to make him bitter or cynical. But, as an artist, he forced himself to deal with issues he had skirted or laughed off in his earlier work. He resolved issues; he took them to their logical conclusions. Not all the pat, formula answers of his earlier films are gone, but in these two wonderful movies we meet a Charlie more closely related to the real world than we have ever met before.

In most of Chaplin's early comedies, the story told in the film was like the "theme" in a vaudeville show: it was a sort of clothesline from which a series of gags, or bits of business, was hung. In *The Pawnshop*, for example, the wonderful sequence when Charlie takes apart the alarm clock does not really advance the story; it adds nothing to the "plot," which is pretty thin anyway. In fact, the story exists only to give Charlie an opportunity to perform the various bits.

In serious drama, the story is more important. In the very best drama, every scene, every sequence, and every turn of events contributes something to the telling of the story. The parts cannot be hung one after another from a line; they must, rather, fit together to form a whole, something like the pieces of a jigsaw puzzle. The way the parts fit together forms the "structure" of the work.

From the start of his career in movies, Chaplin gradually had been paying more and more attention to structure. *A Dog's Life, Shoulder Arms, The Kid,* and *The Pilgrim,* four of the movies he made between 1918 and 1923, were much more carefully constructed than the earlier two-reelers. But not until *A Woman of Paris* did Chaplin learn to relate virtually every part of a film to the film as a whole. And after that he was anxious to apply what he had learned to the making of comedies.

Chaplin did not wish to abandon the wonderful bits of business that were Charlie's stock-in-trade. But when he made *The Gold Rush*, which was released in 1925, he attempted to make these bits contribute to the strength of the whole story. The film contains examples of Charlie's familiar art at its absolute peak. These are not necessarily better than the things Charlie had done before; they are unique because they fit so perfectly into the whole of the film. They are not only terrific bits of business; they are structural elements that advance the story of *The Gold Rush*.

The Gold Rush differs from earlier films, too, in its portrayal of characters. Previously the people with whom the Tramp had to deal were caricatures. The people in *The Gold Rush* are unusually realistic—as realistic as in most dramas. There are no too-dear-to-be-true women here, and even the villain seems human. Furthermore, Charlie establishes and sustains a close friendship with a man—something he hadn't done before—and follows his relationship with a woman to a realistic conclusion.

Many critics consider *The Gold Rush* the best of all Chaplin films, and even those who prefer *City Lights* or some other picture tend to agree that *The Gold Rush* has the best structure.

The Gold Rush takes place in the Klondike, that freezing, barren, snow-covered territory in Alaska and northwest Canada where, in 1886, gold was discovered. Adventurous men made their way through that forbidden land to prospect for precious ore. Only the heartiest survived. Among the brave who gave it a try was a lone prospector called Charlie.

During a storm Charlie finds himself in a cabin with two other prospectors. The villainous one, Larsen, leaves to look for food. Slowly Charlie and his new friend, Big Jim McKay, begin to break under the torture of hunger. Charlie gets an idea, and here he has the opportunity to pantomime his mastery of stylish manners. He decides to cook his shoe. Charlie goes to work with all the finesse of a master chef; he stirs and pokes and tastes until at last the shoe is "done." Delicately Charlie removes it from the pot. Carefully, elegantly, he separates the upper part of the shoe from the heel and sole. He has acted with such precision of form that Big Jim is carried away by the charade; he insists on the upper part of the shoe for himself. Fine with me, Charlie says, and they eat. Charlie twists the shoestrings around his fork and lowers them into his mouth—spaghetti! One by one he removes the nails and sucks their juice, as if they were lobster claws or chicken bones. He even extends one bent nail so that Big Jim can pull the other end—ah! the wishbone. Then Charlie devours the succulent leather itself. It is all done so beautifully and so properly that in a sense the form of cooking and eating becomes more important than what is being cooked and eaten. Anything so well prepared and so handsomely presented *must* be good to eat.

When the storm lets up, the two men, friends for life for having shared the ordeal, split up and go out to search for gold. Charlie finds his way to a mining town. He stops in at the saloon. One look at beautiful Georgia, the dance-hall girl, and Charlie is in love. But Georgia does not even notice Charlie, not even when he stands right next to her.

One day Georgia and the other dance-hall girls, out for a frolic in the snow, come upon Charlie's borrowed cabin, and Charlie invites them to have New Year's Eve dinner with him. To his great joy they accept.

Of course, such a dinner will cost money. Charlie has not forgotten the business methods he employed in *The Kid*. He can't mend windows up here, but he can shovel snow. He gets his first customer and shovels all the snow off his walk—and onto the walk of the house next door. Then he knocks on the door of that house, points to the piled-up snow, and gets a job shoveling that. He clears it onto the walk of the next house and continues down the street.

New Year's Eve. The food is cooking. The table is set beautifully; a "lace" tablecloth made of torn-up newspaper makes everything look elegant. On each girl's plate there is a small, prettily wrapped gift. Charlie waits—and waits—and waits—and he falls asleep. He dreams that the lovely girls are there, delighted with the food and gifts, laughing and enjoying themselves and his charming company. Now to entertain them. This problem is solved by Charlie's second display of flawless pantomime. He sticks two forks into two oval breadrolls, holds the handles of the two forks in one hand under his chin, and, while humming a tune, he makes the breadrolls dance. He becomes a cartoon character with a giant head, no torso, forks for legs, and breadrolls for feet. It is an exquisite dance, so graceful and wonderful that it embodies and radiates all the genius of Charlie Chaplin. Nobody else could have turned a few twists of two forks and two breadrolls into a poetic dance about love and loneliness, dreamy happiness and worldly disappointment, imagined joy and real sadness. It is so simple, and it lasts only a few moments, but they are among the most very special moments ever put on film. Movie audiences spontaneously applaud at the end of the dance of the breadrolls.

He wakes up from his dream, all alone. His expression encloses his whole body. It is almost no expression at all. He looks around the room; his shoulders drop just a little; his eyes scarcely flicker; yet they are windows into his disappointment—a disappointment experienced a dozen times in a dozen films before, an old disappointment but a new hurt every time. He bundles up and walks into town. He stands outside the saloon, looking in. All the girls are there, and Georgia, and all the young men, celebrating the arrival of the New Year. He walks on through the snow.

Meanwhile, Big Jim has been looking for Charlie. Larsen is dead, and word has it that he stashed his gold near the cabin. Big Jim and Charlie find it. They are millionaires!

Dressed like the perfect gentlemen they have become, the partners board ship for home. When Charlie tells reporters about his former life as a mere tramp, a photographer asks him to pose in his old tramp clothes. Graciously Charlie agrees. He steps out on deck, takes a few backward steps, and falls into a coiled rope on a lower deck. Seated beside the rope is Georgia, also bound for home. She thinks Charlie is a tramp stowaway and offers to help him hide. But the captain appears and explains that Charlie, despite his crumby attire, is a millionaire. Georgia is amazed and impressed. Charlie proposes marriage, and Georgia accepts. Then the ship sails off to a wonderful tomorrow of wealth and love.

The happy ending of *The Gold Rush* is not ironic. Georgia, after all, is no sweet and innocent Edna. She wasn't up there in the freezing Klondike for her health. She was a dance-hall girl, probably hoping to link up with a prospector who'd struck it rich. A hundred lovingly prepared dinners could not have won

Georgia's love; by offering her a life of wealth, Charlie won it in an instant. It is not an idealistic ending, just a logical one. Charlie himself isn't fooled. He knows that Georgia's love comes with a price tag. Because he loves her, he is willing to pay it. And since he is able to pay it, the end of *The Gold Rush* makes sense.

The Gold Rush is a completely self-contained work. In the larger view of Charlie's life-on-film, however, it was not as realistic as it might have been. In his feature-length films, Chaplin tried to come to grips with the reality of Charlie's personality. But the fact was that it was unrealistic for Charlie to strike it rich in the Klondike. Like ordinary little people everywhere, Charlie the Tramp would remain essentially what he was. If he was truly the "one universal man of modern times," he would have to get by on his own resources, without benefit of pots of gold.

In *The Circus* (1928), Charlie falls in love with Merna Kennedy, a soft, sweet, vulnerable woman. *The Circus* is a lovely movie, filled with very funny business and a succession of touching moments. But it did not—could not—go any further than *The Tramp* and *The Bank* in resolving Charlie's longing for the love of a woman. Merna is in love with Rex, the high-wire acrobat. The lovers are separated, and Charlie sees how miserable the separation makes Merna. He helps them to get together again and to get married. Selflessly, Charlie has helped make Merna happy—but he is left alone and as miserable as before.

So Chaplin needed something else. Somehow Charlie's idealistic love for a woman must be made to stir feelings greater than mere kindness in the heart of his beloved. His love did not necessarily have to be returned in kind, but at least that possibility must exist. If not, the Tramp as lover would be predictable, in a rut. And such a Tramp would not be interesting—or, for that matter, sympathetic—indefinitely. There comes a time when people stop sympathizing with a man who constantly, time and time again, subjects himself to the exact same suffering.

No, Charlie had everything now—a history, a personality, depth of character. Chaplin knew it was time for Charlie to confront a new experience. Not just a new adventure—there could be nothing newer than being a prospector in the Klondike, certainly—but a new experience of the heart. It was time for his history to apply itself, for his personality to assert itself, for the depth of his character to be measured and put to the test. Whatever was coming would have to be the experience of a lifetime.

13

Say That I Despise Them

Although he was at the peak of his creative powers during the 1920s, the decade was a difficult one for Chaplin. Most of his problems were personal. But toward the end of the decade there was a professional crisis, too: sound came to the movies.

A motion-picture sound track is a length of tape—something like the tape used in modern cartridges and cassettes—attached to one side of the film. Sound-equipped projectors are fitted with devices that pick up and amplify the recorded sound. As the film runs through it, the projector simultaneously plays the tape and projects the picture.

The key word in that description is "simultaneously." For years technicians had known how sound tracks would work; their problem was to develop a system that perfectly synchronized the sound and image. The slam had to be heard precisely when the door was closed; the actor's "Oh!" had to come out at the very moment his mouth formed a circle. Recording tape moved at one speed, however, and film moved at another. Early recording tape was made of wax, which had to move much faster than today's supersentitive plastic tapes to avoid distorting the sound. When the wax tape was attached to movie film, which moved at a speed of sixteen frames per second, it went through the projector at a corresponding rate of four inches per second—much too slow.

There was no magic to the invention of talkies, no uncovering of secrets. All it took was constant improvement of materials and equipment, constant fiddling with ratios, constant experimentation. The process had begun early in the century but did not really get going until the 1920s. Eventually the technicians came up with the theoretical solution, but even when they had that, they needed several more years to make it work.

Part one of the solution was speeding up the shooting and projecting rate of movie film to twenty-four frames per second. Part two of the solution was to make the sound track wavy instead of straight. As a result it was possible for, say, two inches of film to carry along three inches of sound track.

By 1926 sound tracks carrying music and background sound effects were available on some films, but not until the following year did any producer try to record synchronized dialogue. Even then only desperation led Warner Brothers to take the plunge. On the brink of bankruptcy, Warners invested every cent they had and could borrow and made *The Jazz Singer* starring Al Jolson.

The Jazz Singer was a silent movie for the most part, with the usual printed dialogue, but when the great entertainer opened his mouth to sing, out came song! After he finished one song, Jolson spoke to his mother—the first spoken dialogue on screen. The little scene was not even scripted: Jolson simply told her how nice it was to see her and how he wanted to take her out for a bit of fun, maybe to Coney Island. The very clumsiness of the scene contributed to the sense of intimacy. It gave the audience a sense of overhearing a playful conversation between son and mother. A rustle of excitement swept through the theater. After that scene *The Jazz Singer* fell apart. The dramatic story resumed; the printed words returned to the screen, and it didn't seem to be right at all. After hearing words, the audience couldn't readjust to the clumsiness of reading words.

The Jazz Singer was phenomenally successful; it saved Warner Brothers. And since Warners was the only studio with sound equipment, it saved itself many more times throughout 1928. Its head start was quite brief, but it was enough to take Warner Brothers from near bankruptcy to a position among the five major movie producers in one year's time.

At first the other studios took the attitude that talkies were just a passing fad; none wanted to spend the money to convert to sound equipment. But the alternative to not spending the money was to let Warner Brothers be the only company to enjoy the profits of this enormously popular advance in movies. By early 1929 all Hollywood resistance to sound crumbled, and the era of the talkies began.

"You can say that I despise them," Chaplin told a reporter who asked him what he thought of talkies. "Overnight," he wrote later, the motion-picture business became "a cold and serious industry. Sound technicians were renovating studios and building elaborate sound devices. Cameras the size of a room lumbered about the stage like juggernauts. Elaborate radio equipment was installed, involving thousands of electrical wires. Men geared like warriors from Mars sat with earphones while the actors performed with microphones hovering above them like fishing rods. It was all very complicated and depressing. How could anyone be creative with all that junk around?"

Nevertheless, as sound tracks became available, Chaplin used them, cleverly, but modestly, at first. He used sound effects in his next film, *City Lights*—a pair of pompous figures make speeches at the beginning of the film, and their words come out as a squeaky "nyeh-nyeh, nyeh-neh-neh-nyeh," indicating that whatever they were really saying couldn't have been much more meaningful than gibberish. In a brilliant later scene, Charlie, at a party, swallows a whistle. Just as a guest begins to give a brief singing concert, Charlie gets the hiccoughs. Well, not exactly hiccoughs—rather, hic-whistles. The poor man can't sing his song, so finally Charlie considerately goes outside—where his hic-whistles immediately draw every dog in the neighborhood. Charlie rushes back in the house, and the singer is swamped in a canine sea.

Most important, Chaplin took advantage of sound to compose the musical scores for his movies. He provided the music not only for all of his sound films, but also, later for *The Gold Rush*. (In 1942 he removed the printed titles and provided a sound-track narration with himself as storyteller.) Since Chaplin did not know how to score music, he simply used a record-making machine which he sang into. This was not as simple as it may sound:

he had to make sure that the length of his tunes and their mood fit the length and mood of the scenes. Then a professional musician was hired to transcribe the score from record to musical notations.

The nicest thing about Chaplin's music is that it really is very Chaplin-ish. The very same qualities that characterize Charlie's personality and the stories of the movies are present in the music: now it is nervous and frantic, next playful and sweet, then dreamy and wistful, finally melancholy. This harmony of character and music should come as no surprise, of course; composer Chaplin was Chaplin after all. But it is a little surprising anyway, if for no other reason than it is further proof of the man's extraordinary genius. That he could compose music at all is another testament to his versatility. That that music should suit his films so perfectly reveals, again, the wholeness of his vision. He was the master of every aspect of his art and never lost sight of the whole to which every aspect belonged and fitted perfectly.

14

Tomorrow the Birds Will Sing

In *City Lights* Chaplin tells the story of the most important event in Charlie's life. All that the little fellow had done before colors his behavior in this movie. Old themes are explored again, old bits of business refined and repeated, old ideas clarified and restated. In a way *City Lights* is a summing up of all the "Tramp" movies.

But in another way *City Lights* is unique. As *The Gold Rush* was the most carefully constructed of all Chaplin's films, *City Lights* is the most believable. In the past we, the viewers, willingly suspended our belief in the natural order of things. Many of the situations in which we found Charlie were clearly foolish, but who cared? The bits of business were funny, and the messages had the ring of truth. In *City Lights*, however, we are not asked to suspend our belief in logical order. Every episode of plot and subplot is taken to its reasonable conclusion. And, after the opening pair of sequences, every episode is related to the plot.

In his early movie *The Champion*, Chaplin had put Charlie into a boxing ring because a boxing ring was handy. After two fights, Charlie won the championship. And that was fine back then: the plot was simply a vehicle for short messages and funny bits. But when Charlie returns to the ring in *City Lights*, his being there is explained reasonably.

Similarly, we never questioned Edna's love for the Tramp in the films with happy endings. If Chaplin said that a desirable, beautiful young woman was in love with a clown-footed vagabond,

94

it was all right with us. But in *City Lights* a relationship develops between the Tramp and a beautiful young woman logically. It is as if Chaplin asked: Under what circumstances might a lovely woman love a shabby tramp? and then answered: If she doesn't know that he's a tramp. This is precisely the case in *City Lights*.

In all of the earlier films we're not quite sure how the story will end, and we don't really care. In some of them Edna marries Charlie; in others she turns out to have another lover. But because *City Lights* presents a believable story, its ending does matter. As we watch the movie, we are drawn into the reasonableness of the situations. We expect a reasonable outcome. And that's just what we get—although, when we get it, we may not be too happy about it.

City Lights tells two stories. One describes the on-again, off-again friendship between Charlie and a millionaire. The other is about Charlie's love for a beautiful blind flower girl. Although the stories are told in separate sequences, they are related to each other and combine at the end of the movie.

(One way that Chaplin made interesting use of sound was to weave the two stories together with music. The score of *City Lights* contains several different melodies, and one of them represents the flower girl. In the scene where Charlie first meets the millionaire and the two men go off together, Charlie picks up the flower he had bought from the flower girl that day, and the flower-girl melody plays. The audience knows that he is thinking of her because of the tune.)

Charlie meets the millionaire at the riverbank, where the rich man, who is drunk, has come to commit suicide. Charlie comforts him. "Tomorrow the birds will sing!" he tells him through a printed title. Convinced, finally, that life is precious, the millionaire declares that he and Charlie will be friends for life. The trouble is, the millionaire knows Charlie only when he is drunk. One night he gives Charlie his Rolls-Royce car. In the morning, however, sobered up, he has no idea who Charlie is. Get away from my car, he gestures, and drives off. Later, drunk again, the millionaire stumbles into Charlie: "My friend!" And he takes Charlie home and throws a big party. In the morning the two men wake up in the millionaire's bed. Now sober again, the millionaire rings for the butler. "Who is this man?" he asks. "Throw him out!"

Charlie's love for the flower girl is his reason for living in *City Lights*. Early in the film he uses his last coin to buy a flower from her. When she becomes ill, Charlie gets a job as a street cleaner so that he can take her groceries. Every day at lunch hour he visits the girl and reads to her. She thinks he is very rich, and of course she loves him for all his kindness.

One day, in the girl's tiny apartment, Charlie finds a letter saying that she and her grandmother will be evicted if they do not pay the twenty-dollar rent. Don't worry, he tells the girl, he'll pay it. He also reads a newspaper story telling of a doctor in Vienna who has found a cure for the kind of blindness that afflicts the girl. He says nothing about the story to her, but the thoughtful expression on his face tells us that he will find a way to pay for her trip to Vienna. Unfortunately, Charlie has spent so much of his lunch hour comforting the girl about the rent that he is late returning to work and is fired. Now he is worse off than before. When he walks past a seedy fight club, a tough stops him, suggesting they be partners. The prize money in this club is fifty dollars, winner take all, but the fighter wants the two of them to take it easy with each other and split the purse in half. Charlie agrees; with his twenty-five dollars he can at least pay the girl's rent. But this really is Charlie's unlucky day. The fighter suddenly gets a message that the cops are after him, and he flees. His replacement, a bigger and tougher fighter, won't keep the deal.

The prizefight itself is a masterpiece of dancing. Charlie uses the referee as a barrier between himself and his huge opponent. His footwork is so quick and rhythmic that the referee and the fighter start dancing, keeping time. Charlie is setting the pace; so he is able to interrupt the rhythm to land a couple of good punches. Most of the fight is sidesplittingly funny. But in keeping with the overall spirit of *City Lights*, it ends as it must end— with Charlie knocked out cold. And not one cent to show for it!

Although the two stories of *City Life* are quite serious, Chaplin included some of his funniest bits of business in this film. When Charlie and the millionaire get smashingly drunk, they go to a nightclub where they can't tell the difference between paper streamers and spaghetti and eat both. Heading for home, the millionaire drives his huge Rolls-Royce insanely—up on sidewalks, in and out of trolley lanes, faster and faster. Charlie shouts, "Be careful how you're driving!" The millionaire bobs his head, tries to focus on Charlie, and says, "Am I driving?"

In the dressing room scene before the prizefight, another fighter rubs a horseshoe and a rabbit's foot all over himself for luck before he goes out to fight. Charlie rubs the horseshoe and rabbit's foot all over himself, too, for luck. An instant later, the superstitious fighter is brought back in—on a stretcher. Charlie looks at him and tries to rub *off* the effect of the good-luck charms.

The millionaire is one of the most complex characters ever to appear in a Chaplin film. He is rich and lonely and miserable. Sober he is cold and hard. Drunk he is not exactly Mr. Warmth, but he is at least loose enough to appreciate Charlie's tenderness. Even so, he is only buying Charlie's friendship. Money is the only thing he knows how to give.

Another very well drawn character is the millionaire's butler. This butler is one of those servants—more typical in English drama than American—who is a much greater snob than his employer. The millionaire, when he is drunk, draws no class distinction between himself and the Tramp. But the butler does. He sees Charlie as a ragamuffin vagabond; no matter that he is making the millionaire's miserable life tolerable. When Charlie enters the house, the butler, behind his employer's back, forbids Charlie to so much as sit on the sofa.

After the prizefight, Charlie heads downtown. He is broke, worried, and sad. He wants to help the girl to regain her eyesight, but now he can't even pay her rent. He walks past a theater. There, staggering drunk, is the millionaire. He is delighted to see his old friend. Charlie tells him about the flower girl's plight, and the millionaire snaps his fingers: nothing to it! He'll provide the money.

Charlie and the millionaire unknowingly enter the millionaire's mansion while it is being burglarized. After the millionaire hands Charlie the money, one of the thieves knocks the millionaire out. The police arrive to find Charlie holding more than a thousand dollars in cash. But before they can grab him, Charlie escapes.

He hurries to the flower girl's home. Pressing some cash into each of her hands, he explains, "This is for the rent, and this is for your eyes." How can she ever thank him? Charlie imitates the millionaire's gesture; he snaps his fingers: nothing to it. Knowing that he will probably be sent to jail, he tells the girl that he will have to be going away for a while. They part, she filled with gratitude, he filled with happiness that she will be cured and with sorrow at their parting.

Charlie is arrested on a street corner that figures prominently in *City Lights*. He passes it several times during the film, and each time he is confronted by a pair of devilish newsboys. Perhaps twelve or fourteen years old, these boys torture the life out of Charlie. Whenever they see him approaching, they begin to laugh, whistle, call out insults, and imitate his funny walk. When he passes, they try to steal his hat or cane. The newsboys are poor. You can tell from their worn shoes and threadbare clothes. Charlie, however, is poorer than they are, and not only is he poorer—he is ridiculous. So when they see him, the boys feel good. He reminds them, with his absurd formal attire, that although they are poor, they are not ridiculous. The more ridiculous they make him seem, the better they feel.

This time as Charlie approaches their corner, the newsboys' tormenting is interrupted by two police officers. When they grab him, Charlie drops his cane. The newsboys rush over. They begin defending Charlie. The policemen move to take Charlie away. But before they go, the boys pick up the cane and give it back to the Tramp.

Before, Charlie had been a foolish figure, a figure of fun. Now he is in trouble. They do not know why he is being arrested. They don't have to know. They know only that he is a gentle, harmless soul being led away in shame in public. When they give him back his cane, they are giving him back his dignity.

Later, they will see Charlie again, and again they will torment him. For that, says Chaplin, is human nature—capable of cruelty and kindness, monumental insensitivity, great sensitivity, and monumental insensitivity again.

While Charlie is in jail, the flower girl goes to Vienna and has the operation. We know that it has been successful because as the final sequence of *City Lights* begins, we see her and her grandmother and a helper in a florist's shop near the newsboys' corner. We know that she can see because she looks in a mirror and primps her hair. She is a complete woman now, beautiful and full of laughter and proud of her beauty.

Along with Georgia of *The Gold Rush*, the flower girl is the most reasonable of Charlie's beloveds. She is innocent and fragile, and her love for Charlie seems believable because of her blindness, because she has experienced his gentleness and generosity, and because she has no way of knowing that he is a tramp. She wonders about him to her grandmother, who has never seen him. "He must be very rich," the grandmother says. "He must be very handsome," says the girl. He must indeed; any man who does so much for a woman, asking nothing in return, could not be anything but handsome. She thinks of him constantly after her vision has been restored.

As the three women in the flower shop straighten up the place, the camera takes us around the corner. Here comes Charlie, out of jail at last. He has never looked so shabby. He has no shirt under his ragged jacket, and his precious walking cane is gone. His hands are in his bottomless pockets, and though it does not seem to be a cool day, he is shivering. He turns the corner and tolerates the abuses of the newsboys.

While the boys torment him, the helper whisks the sweepings from the flower shop floor outside into the gutter. The Tramp sees part of a flower lying in the debris and picks it up. He has always loved flowers; his time in jail has not spoiled that. He stands up straight, turns, and sees the flower girl through the shop window. He stares for a few seconds, focusing his eyes on hers, making certain that she is no longer blind. The girl looks back at him and laughs. "I've made a conquest!" she says. My, my, a tramp who likes flowers! The girl holds up a fresh, untorn flower, offering it to the Tramp. He does not respond; so the girl offers him a quarter, too. The offer registers, and the Tramp starts to move on. The flower girl, still smiling, goes after him: Here you are, you funny little man, her gesture says, take it, go ahead. She reaches out and takes his hand and puts the coin and flower in it.

All her life the girl was blind; all her life she learned to recognize things by their feel. She feels Charlie's hand. Recognition registers by degrees. She looks quizzically into his eyes. Her smile fades. An almost tortured cloud crosses her face. She looks at this poor, ridiculous figure of a man, smiling his shy smile with his finger in his mouth, a flower in front of his face, and she knows. And what is more agonizing, he knows, too. He knows, for the first time ever, how ridiculous he is. His expression is so intense that it radiates pain to all who look at it. It is, as the writer Robert Payne has put it, "a face so terrible and beautiful that you . . . almost wish you never set eyes upon him." And James Agee wrote of it: "It is enough to shrivel the heart to see, and it is the greatest piece of acting and the highest moment in movies."

"You can see now?" Charlie asks his beloved flower girl. And the flower girl brings the movie to a close with words that refer to more than her eyesight:

"Yes, I can see."

She can see. She can see that a poor vagabond clown has loved her, and sacrificed for her, and traded parts of his freedom and his very life so that her life could be complete. She can see that the man she's loved for what he's done for her is a man she can never love for himself. And she probably can see that he doesn't really expect her to give him the sort of love he has given her.

And that is why *City Lights* tells the story of the greatest experience in the life of the Tramp. He has chosen to be anonymous. He pretended, after all, that he was a millionaire. Nothing to it! he had snapped with his fingers. By posing as a rich and charitable man, he relieved some of the girl's gratitude. Had she known the truth—had she known that he had swept the streets to buy her groceries, stepped into a boxing ring in an effort to raise her rent money, gone to jail to pay for her eyesight—she would have been so deeply indebted that her only repayment would have been herself. But Charlie does not ask that; he does not expect it. If he wanted her for himself he would have continued the masquerade—and kept her blind. He gave her back her vision because he loved her and wanted her to be a complete woman. Why waste a complete woman on a shabby tramp? That expression of his at the end—that contains the realization that he is a waste, a man unworthy to be paired with so lovely a woman.

In countless previous movies the Tramp had suffered when his Ednas went off with their handsome lovers. In a few he had sacrificed his own happiness for that of his beloved. But never before has he dedicated his very existence to the benefit of a girl. Never before has he made such personal sacrifices to secure a goal which, once secured, could only result in his own heartbreak. In *City Lights* Charlie so dedicates himself and makes that ultimate sacrifice. He has always been a poor, shabby, ridiculous clown, pure of heart, wonderfully spirited, but not really suited to live the conventional life on this earth. He has always been an outcast, and now he knows it. The realization comes at the end of *City Lights*, but he must have known all along. Deep down he has always known it.

15

We'll Get Along

City Lights was a great success, but its making had been exhausting. After the openings, Chaplin took a year-long trip around the world. When he returned to Hollywood late in 1932, he had to decide what—if anything—to do next. Should he make another movie, or should he retire?

In favor of retirement was the fact that he was rich and still relatively young—forty-three. He had liked China and thought of settling there. Against retirement was his urge to work, and to continue speaking out, through his work, on the issues that concerned him. Moreover, while he was trying to make up his mind about what to do, he met Paulette Goddard, a beautiful and intelligent young actress from New York. Secretly—for he had had his fill of publicity—they were married in 1933. Paulette had a wonderful vitality and a down-to-earth sincerity that Chaplin thought would come across well on screen. And her personality was not like Edna's, or the Mabel-Georgia-type leading lady, but something in between—innocent but at the same time tough. Chaplin thought that she would be an interesting new companion for the Tramp.

And finally, Chaplin had been brooding about a criticism of *City Lights*. Although almost every major motion-picture critic had applauded that fine film, more than one had commented on its sentimentality. A poor tramp dedicating his life to a blind flower girl is a pitiful situation and bound to produce tears. One critic suggested that Chaplin should now try to create a realistic situation in which to place the Tramp—a situation with which people in the audience were familiar.

Chaplin recalled a discussion he had with a newspaper reporter who told him about the assembly lines of Detroit. In assembly-line manufacturing, a product is made quickly and in great numbers. The process takes place along conveyor belts. In Detroit the product is an automobile, but the system is used for all mass-produced products. As a rule, the worker on an assembly line has one and only one job to do. According to the reporter, men were coming from the farms to work on the assembly lines, but after four or five years of that monotony, they became nervous wrecks.

The assembly line, a symbol of modern times, of the age of industry, appealed to Chaplin as an idea for a film. He had always been concerned about the dignity of the individual. The assembly line was a great insult to that dignity. For a worker on the line was merely a piece of machinery; he fit a piece of metal into a groove or bolted two parts together or tightened nuts. He was not really making anything himself; he could feel no pride in the finished product. He simply repeated one small motion over and over again all day long.

The well-meaning Tramp had always resisted insults to his dignity. He had never been able to go along with the crowd, to do what was expected of him just to earn his daily bread. Now Chaplin would introduce the Tramp to an enemy stronger and more oppressive than any cop or waiter. He would create a confrontation between the Tramp and the machine age.

Unlike Chaplin's other feature-length films, *Modern Times* does not have a tight structure. Its story is more like that old clothesline, something to hang sequences from. In fact it is sort of like three two-reelers, each with its own theme. The first two-reeler, the first one-third of the movie, stands pretty much on its own, completely self-contained and brilliant. The themes of the second and third two-reelers are woven together; the fabric is whole, but the strands are distinctly different.

The themes are not new to Charlie. They are work, society, and love. But Chaplin's view of and approach to the themes are very different from what they had been in the days of the Essanay and Mutual two-reelers. And no wonder: times had changed.

Charlie had always been a man of his times, but in *Modern Times* his relationship to the era in which he lives seems closer than it had ever been before. This should not be at all surprising. Charlie had always been an outsider, and that made him seem unusual. By the time *Modern Times* was released, the world had passed through the deepest, darkest days of the Great Depression. Although unemployment was not as severe as it had been early in the 1930s, the Depression had not released its grip easily. For many people it was still very much a fact of life in 1936, when *Modern Times* was released. And even those whose fortunes had gradually improved had learned a lesson. They felt disillusioned by society. Those who had known months and years of unemployment had learned what it meant to be an outsider. The gap between themselves and Charlie had closed somewhat. Charlie was much less unusual than he had once been.

When the gloomiest Depression clouds began to lift in 1933 and 1934, many workers experienced the attacks on their dignity that had always plagued the Tramp. Owners of factories and other businesses knew that there were more unemployed men than there were jobs for them, and they took advantage of the situation. They paid low wages, demanded long hours, and did little if anything to create decent working conditions for laborers. If a worker had any objection, he could quit; there were plenty of men waiting for his job, he was told. One way for workers to protect themselves was to form a labor union. In the United States, President Franklin D. Roosevelt's administration supported the right of labor to organize unions, and Congress backed up that support with laws. But it took a long time for the effects of federal legislation to work their way down to the local level. Very often factory owners convinced local leaders and police that workers were being organized by so-called communists and other subversives. Those were magic demon-words. The police and the National Guard were sent in to break the only tool the workingman had to guarantee his rights—the strike. Conflicts between local authority and labor unionists were commonplace during the thirties. Many were the workers who felt the oppressiveness of authority bearing down, crushing their hopes and ambitions and trust in society. Under that weight, it became easier to understand what the funny little Tramp had been trying to stand up to for years.

The Charlie of *Modern Times* is different from the earlier Charlie whose life's struggles had been summed up in *City Lights*. It is not that he has abruptly given up one sort of life to assume another. He has changed because the times have changed him, as they have changed almost everybody. He seems less an outsider because so many more are outsiders. He regards society differently because society has changed: the threat to his happiness is no longer the Idle Class, but the Managerial Class. Even his approach to love has changed, partly because, after the experience of *City Lights*, he would have been stupid to keep looking for another Edna. But the times were partly responsible for his changing approach to love, too; for the times helped to create his new partner.

Work, society, even love has changed, and Charlie changes with them. He retains his good nature, his good humor, his incredible gracefulness, and his tender heart; but as he smiles, teases, waddles, runs, marches, tumbles, dances, roller-skates, dreams, loves, and—yes—sings his way through the three themes of *Modern Times*, he is every inch a creature of the Great Depression.

Stagehand, farmhand, paperhanger, janitor, fireman, pawnshop clerk, waiter, prizefighter, police officer, soldier, window mender, prospector, snow shoveler, street sweeper: Charlie hadn't exactly excelled at the jobs he held in his earlier films, but at least they were jobs. Even if he bungled them, he knew what it was he was bungling. And thanks to an occasional accidental slip in the right direction he at times did something right and found momentary pleasure. My, how things had changed.

Modern Times begins with shots of machinery—gigantic machinery, a collection of colossal wheels and pulleys and gears. What is that machinery doing? Moving, And why is it moving? It is making something. And what is it making? Who knows?

Does it matter? The men working alongside the wheels and conveyer belts certainly don't have to know. All they do is add something or turn something or tighten something, the same gesture, over and over again. They are only parts of the machinery. What does it matter, the film seems to say, to a man whose job it is to turn a screw a thousand times an hour whether he is making a tractor or a radio?

Now we meet the boss of the factory. With a control panel on his desk, the boss can watch what's happening in any part of the factory on a closed-circuit television screen. At the same time, his enormously magnified face appears on screens throughout the place.

Chaplin decided to use the sound track for speech in *Modern Times*, but the way he used it is significant. The only real voices we hear come through machines. For example, the boss booms out his orders to the factory workers only through loudspeakers. An inventor, selling the boss a machine to feed workers on the assembly line (so that they won't have to pause for lunch), doesn't give the sales talk himself; he plays a record that explains the wonders of the machine. When people in the film talk face-to-face, their words are printed onscreen, as in silent movies. The sum of this is that the audience never hears a direct human voice, only voices distorted and amplified through electronic devices—the factory loudspeakers, the salesman's phonograph record, and, later, a radio. This use of sound is quite in keeping with the message of *Modern Times*. In the factory the machines are more important than the men who stand beside them and work; the men themselves are only human cogs in the great cogs and wheels. In such a machine world things like human relationships and human communication become insignificant. The fact that we hear only machine-voices in *Modern Times* symbolizes the ultimate horror—a world where only machinery talks and humanity stands mute.

The machinery moves; the assembly line flows; and there, a wrench in each hand, tightening a pair of nuts on a flat metal plate, is Charlie, dressed in overalls. He seems to be pretty good at what he's doing. But wait—a problem. Charlie has an itch under his arm. He takes a split second to scratch with a wrench and in that split second the whole rhythm of the assembly line is ruined. One or two plates slip by with their nuts untightened. Before the plates disappear into a machine tunnel, Charlie has to rush down the line. The other men on the line are yelling at him. But he makes it: he tightens the missed nuts in time. Back at his place, he tightens nuts faster to catch up and restore the proper rhythm. A while later, Charlie goes to the lavatory. He steps back from the conveyor belt, but he cannot stop the twisting movement of his wrists. As he walks toward the lavatory, he continues tightening invisible nuts. Finally he grits his teeth and gets together all his strength, stretches his arms stiffly outward, and stops wrenching. In the lavatory he pauses for a smoke. But suddenly the giant screen on the lavatory wall lights up with the face of the boss. Hey, you! the loudspeaker yells; get back to work! Is there no privacy in this modern world? Can't a man even take a smoke in a men's room without being spied on? Apparently not. Charlie returns to the boredom of the assembly line. The boss orders another speedup of the belt. When Charlie says something to the man beside him, he misses another couple of plates. This time the plates go into the machine before he can catch up. In panic, Charlie dives into the tunnel after the plates. Now we see him passing over and under wheels and gears, a modern man swallowed up by modern machinery. The foreman reverses the machine to get Charlie out. No one asks him if he is hurt; everyone scolds him for slowing down the assembly line. Back to work. Back to the same wrenching boredom until, at last, lunchtime comes.

Lunchtime brings a new torture of modern technology to the factory. The inventor has persuaded the boss to try his feeding machine. If the machine works, the factory will not have to stop for lunch: the men can continue to work while they eat.

The boss selects Charlie for the demonstration. Charlie stands at the belt; the inventor wheels the machine in place.

The machine first lifts a bowl of soup to his mouth and tilts it slightly; but Charlie has not even finished with the first course when the machine begins to go crazy. It starts moving too quickly.

The inventor can't seem to fix it, although he unfastens nuts and tries to make adjustments. The machine's many arms and feeding devices keep operating as Charlie stands there, helpless. The soup bowl hurls the whole bowlful of soup down the front of Charlie's shirt; the napkin device wipes his mouth. The meat-pusher pushes all the meat—and a couple of iron nuts the inventor mistakenly places on the plate—into Charlie's mouth. Charlie tries to spit them out, but his mouth is blocked by the napkin device. The corn spinner moves in front of his mouth so fast that kernels fly every which way; the napkin wipes his mouth. The cream pie is deposited on Charlie's neck; the napkin wipes his mouth. All the machine's actions get mixed up: kernels of corn, plates, sparks fly, and the napkin keeps wiping Charlie's mouth. Finally the motor blows out altogether, and the machine, with one last dainty wipe of Charlie's mouth, stops. The boss tells the inventor (with printed words, since his voice here is not transmitted electronically) that the machine is not practical. Then it's back to work.

Charlie can't quite recover from the shock of the feeding machine. A woman walks through the factory. On the back of her dress are buttons that resemble the nuts he is supposed to tighten. He looks at her menacingly. She notices and runs away in fear. He runs after her: he is determined to tighten her buttons. She escapes, but Charlie runs wild. He tightens everything in sight. He runs out of the factory; he tightens the nuts on a fire hydrant by the curb. He sees a fat lady walking toward him. On her dress, too, on the bosom, there are two big buttons. Charlie wants to tighten them. He runs after her. She runs into a policeman, who grabs Charlie and takes him back into the factory. Someone takes away his wrenches, but Charlie picks up an oil can. Now that he has tightened everything, he wants to oil everything. He oils the machinery. He oils the men on the assembly line. He oils the foreman. He oils the cop. Finally he is subdued. He is taken away in a patrol wagon to the psychiatric ward of a hospital, for he has suffered a nervous breakdown.

So ends the first section of *Modern Times*. In a way this first half hour—about the length of the old two-reel comedies—is a complete movie in itself. It is, above all, hysterically funny, but it is also a powerful statement about work in the modern world. At its most horrifying, Chaplin was saying, the machine age makes machines of men. And the only reasonable response to such a world—a world that drenches one's shirt with soup and then wipes one's mouth to show its concern for good manners—is to go crazy.

As a sort of punctuation mark to the first section, we see Charlie, now dressed as the Tramp again, after his release from the hospital. As he walks down the street, a lumber truck passes him; its red warning flag falls to the ground. Charlie, ever helpful, picks it up. He moves to the middle of the street, holding the flag aloft, hoping that the driver will see him and come back for his lost flag. At that very instant, a group of striking workers comes around the corner behind Charlie. A second later, policemen on horseback arrive, charge into the strikers, break up their demonstration, and arrest Charlie. For in that moment Charlie, waving a red flag—a communist symbol—appears to be leading the strikers. He is sent to jail as a communist leader! From the psychiatric ward to jail in the same day. What a life!

While Charlie is serving his jail sentence, we meet "the Gamine," played by Paulette Goddard. *Gamine*, a French word, means, loosely, "girl of the streets." She roams the streets stealing food, and eventually runs into Charlie, who's free again. Interestingly, they meet while she is trying to avoid the police and Charlie is trying to get back in prison—at least there he had known where his next meal was coming from. But once they get together, he gives up all notions of returning to jail and spends his time dreaming with the lovely Gamine.

In *Modern Times*, at last, Charlie finds a suitable partner. The Gamine is exactly like Charlie. Just as Spike and Scraps were the dogs that Charlie would have been if he had been a dog, just as the Kid was a junior version of the Tramp, so the Gamine is the female Charlie. She is poor, innocent, filled with the joy of life, trusting, able to survive against all the obstacles that society places in the way of the innocent and trusting.

Charlie and the Gamine are wonderful together; they even have the same middle-class dreams. Resting on a nice suburban street, they daydream of a cozy little home with a fruit tree outside the window, their own cow outside the back door to give them fresh milk, and a fine steak on the stove. After they come out of their pleasant fantasy, Charlie is determined. "We'll get a home," he says, and they go off together to look for work.

Charlie gets a job as a night watchman in a department store. After the store closes, Charlie lets the girl in, and they head straight for the toy department. Charlie entertains the Gamine by putting on a blindfold and doing a lovely dance on roller skates. Charlie does not see that the gate around a balcony over the floor below has been removed. The skating is indescribably beautiful and graceful and funny, but it is horrifying too: time and again the blindfolded Charlie skates right up to the edge of the balcony, only to turn sharply back into the room. The Gamine sees the danger, but she is afraid that if she cries out, she will startle him and he will skate over the edge. Finally the dance ends, and Charlie takes off the blindfold. He sees how close he had come to disaster—and now he almost falls over the edge.

Charlie puts the girl to bed in the softest bed in the bedding department and makes his rounds. In the liquor department he skates right into a burglary. The burglars make him stand against a barrel of rum. One of the guns goes off and shoots a hole in the barrel; rum pours into his mouth. Charlie's life is spared, but he is so drunk that nothing matters to him. In the morning when the store opens, the manager finds him sleeping in the fabrics department. And Charlie is sent to jail once more.

When Charlie is released ten days later, the girl is waiting for him. "I've found a home," she tells him, and takes him to a shack on the waterfront. Horrible as the place is, the Tramp and the Gamine are happy there. One morning Charlie goes off to apply for a job. But soon after he starts working, another worker comes by. "We're on strike," he explains. As the frustrated Charlie leaves the factory, a cop pushes him and tells him to move on. He was in fact moving on in the first place, but the Tramp doesn't like to be pushed. With a simple gesture—his eyebrows raised, his index finger raised—Charlie tells the cop: Okay I'm going, but just don't push. The cop pushes him again. Charlie repeats the gesture. The cop pushes him again. Charlie pushes him back. Jail again.

During his two weeks in jail, the Gamine gets a job dancing in a cafe. When Charlie gets out of jail, the girl, all dressed up in nice clothes bought with her wages, tells him he can have a job as a singing waiter. As a waiter Charlie is a disaster, but the cafe owner is willing to see how well Charlie can sing. Unfortunately, Charlie cannot remember the words to his song, which is about a fat old rich man who tries to win the heart of a pretty young girl. The Gamine thinks of a solution: she writes the words on Charlie's cuffs. When the time comes, Charlie dances out into the cafe. He dances back and forth and throws his arms outward, and the cuffs of his shirt fly away. (On some old-time shirts, cuffs and collars were removable.) Now what will he do? The band is playing his song; he is there onstage with all eyes on him, and he doesn't know the words. He repeats his introductory dance. Then he opens his mouth and . . . for the first time ever, for the first time in more than seventy-five films, we hear the voice of the Tramp.

He sings. He sings in French. In French? How on earth would a Tramp know French? Well, he wouldn't and doesn't. It is entirely fake. "Je poissey potte-beeley," he sings as he makes a round motion with his hands in front of his stomach. It is gibberish, but with a suggestion of potbelly at the end. And so with words that mean nothing and with beautiful pantomime and lovely dance steps, Charlie tells the story of a fat old man and a pretty young girl. The audience loves it; they clap and cheer, and Charlie has to take bow after bow after bow. The excited cafe owner rushes into the dressing room. "You're a hit!" Charlie can have a job for life; he won't even have to wait tables.

The Tramp and the Gamine hug one another. Now they can have that nice pretty home. Now they will be able to eat three good meals a day without having to steal their food, without having to dance in the gutter for pennies, without having to work like a piece of machinery on an assembly line. Now they have a fine future together!

Except for one thing: In the audience are two plainclothes

policemen who have been searching for the Gamine. They barge into the dressing room. There is a brief chase, and the Tramp and the Gamine manage to escape.

In the morning they awaken in the country. They have left the city altogether. The girl is distressed. All their plans have been shattered, all their dreams ruined. Her vitality, her joy in living seem to be gone. She cries, and Charlie tries to comfort her. No words are heard or printed, but we know what he is saying: He is pointing out the beauty of the day, of the flowers, of the sky. He is reminding her that they still have each other. They aren't going to let a couple of cops and a bit of bad luck get them down, are they? They still have their dreams; no one can take them away. They'll live, won't they? They'll still go on dreaming together, won't they? "We'll get along!" the Tramp insists.

The girl lifts her tear-stained face and looks straight ahead. Chaplin's song "Smile," the words of which say, "Smile though your heart is aching," plays on the sound track. The sad expression on the girl's face dissolves; it is replaced with a look of firmness and determination. She lifts her clenched fist and says, "You betcha!"

They get up from the ground, brush themselves off, and step to the middle of the road. The road is long and straight and disappears in the distance. Above the horizon the sun is rising. They hold hands and begin to walk down the road in the direction of the sunrise. They walk slowly, with their heads held high and proud. They are ready for whatever the new day has in store for them.

So ends *Modern Times.*

And so ends the motion-picture story of the Tramp. For as he disappeared down the long road of life, he was beginning his last journey on film. Never again would Charles Chaplin pick up the cane and put on the oversized shoes and pants and the undersized derby hat and cutaway coat to make a movie.

And, all things considered, it is a happy ending. True, the Tramp's simple dreams have not come true. True, society has kicked him around and gotten the best of him again. But the flowers are still growing, and the sun still warms him, and a hundred hopes still crowd his calendar for a hundred tomorrows. He has never turned away from life; he will not turn away now. He faces it as he has always faced it.

And best of all, as he faces life now, he is not alone.

16

Villains

Chaplin's genius was intuitive. He and the medium of motion pictures were ideally suited to each other; he almost always knew, instinctively, what would and what would not work on film. He didn't sit down and think up a theory of acting that was ideal for the screen; he just knew the right way to act. Once he had the mechanics of moviemaking mastered, he became more of a perfectionist. He worked more slowly and with greater deliberation, but when he went to work on a project, he went about it properly. There are no Tramp movies that can be considered really poor, and after 1919 none can be called less than very good; so obviously he knew what he was doing. When, during World War I, he decided to send the Tramp to war, all of his colleagues advised him not to do it: the war, they said, was no subject for a comedy. But his instincts told him to go ahead, and he did, and the result was *Shoulder Arms*, still regarded by some as his greatest film. When he decided to make a feature-length movie and to make it with a mixture of comedy, drama, and tragedy, his friends said that those elements wouldn't mix, and his distributor threatened not to release it. But he listened to his intuition, and he went ahead with it, and the result was *The Kid*, another masterpiece, another with a following that still calls it his best.

And when sound came, everything in Hollywood changed, and everybody knew that silent pictures were through; there was no way on earth that the public would now pay money to see a

Charlie wants to get into *The Circus* (1928).

Caught up in the wheels and gears
of the Machine Age, Charlie temporarily
goes crazy in *Modern Times* (1936).
Chaplin's co-star is Paulette Goddard.

GOOD-BYE, CHARLIE   When the Tramp and his
girl friend walked down the road toward the sunrise at the
end of *Modern Times,* Charlie's life story on film came
to a close. Talking pictures had created a revolution in
movies that Chaplin—who knew that a talking Charlie
could not be everyman—could no longer ignore. During
the next sixteen years—very difficult years for Chaplin,
personally—he made three movies without Charlie.

Chaplin as the little Jewish barber surrounded
by Nazi-like soldiers in *The Great Dictator* (1940).

Monsieur Verdoux (1947)
features Charlie as
a wife-murderer and Martha
Raye as one of his
unsuspecting wives.

A memorable moment on film: Chaplin and his silent-comedy
rival, Buster Keaton, in a scene from *Limelight* (1952).

In 1966 Chaplin directed
Marlon Brando, Sophia Loren,
and his son Sydney (standing
beside him) in *A Countess
from Hong Kong,* the final film
of his fifty-one-year career.

A candle for each decade: Charles Chaplin celebrated
his seventieth birthday at his home
in Switzerland, with his wife Oona, and with Victoria
and Eugene, two of their eight children.

movie that didn't talk. When that happened, Chaplin's inner voice told him to go ahead with *City Lights* as planned, and he listened, and *City Lights* stuck out like a sore thumb in 1931, the only nontalkie released that year. But it played to full houses, and it was and remains the one movie cited most often when people are asked to name Chaplin's greatest film.

But five years later keeping the Tramp voiceless was downright foolhardy; everybody said that. By then the talkies had been perfected; Hollywood was in its prime; the studios were turning out one beautiful movie after another. A silent movie now would be dated. But Chaplin had a feeling that the Tramp should keep quiet in *Modern Times*, and the feeling won over the apparent logic, and *Modern Times* packed them in and earned for itself a place on the list of movies thought to be Chaplin's best.

Then he stopped, or at least he stopped making movies about Charlie. And though he said he just despised talking pictures, one wonders if perhaps, down deep, his intuition told him that it was time to stop. Chaplin did a lot of things correctly during his career, and always he was guided by his instincts. Why not now, too? Intuitively he had known how to act in movies, how to direct, how to make masterpieces. Perhaps now the same intuition told him that Charlie's day was done. He may have known that it was time to leave Charlie to history.

But when he left Charlie to history in 1936, Chaplin left behind his own best defense against the world. An odd thing about the relationship between the public and Charlie and the relationship between the public and Chaplin was that they were separate. People loved Charlie, but Chaplin was not very popular. There always seemed to be somebody around criticizing him for one thing or another.

His refusal to become an American citizen remained an issue, and so did his marriages to two teenaged girls, which offended the puritanical streak in many Americans. Another sore spot was his politics. Although he never belonged to a political party and admired statesmen of various political stripes, Chaplin was, by instinct, a liberal. His boyhood had taught him to despise inequality: there was no excuse, in his mind, for hunger and poverty and workhouses in the rich, modern world. He felt that the first obligation of governments was to see that all people lived in freedom and with dignity. He feared that the machine age would enslave humanity; he was anxious that machines, and the powerful men who built them, be kept in their place—as servants, not masters, of society. He often pointed out in his films that wealth did not make some men smarter than other men—merely wealthier; that power did not make some men wiser than other men—merely more powerful. He believed that in a system based on competitiveness and profit those who succeeded often sacrificed a number of human virtues, including humility and charity. In other words, Chaplin felt—and expressed the idea again and again in his work—that in modern times the world was ruled by those who had the least of the best human virtues. Perhaps this was necessary to make society efficient, but, Chaplin seemed to say, there was more to life than efficiency. In our struggle to survive we must not neglect beauty and dignity and the love and wisdom that reside in the souls of ordinary folk. The world, after all, belongs to them. And if it does not, it should.

Chaplin admired President Franklin D. Roosevelt, and he admired the American people whose greatness, he wrote, was tested and proven during the Great Depression. He also admired Russia's experiment in socialism. He detested the new European dictators, Mussolini and Hitler and Franco, as he detested fascism in all its forms; for nothing, in Chaplin's mind, was worse than a system that forbade people to oppose it. Among his acquaintances were many Communists and Socialists, and when, in the United States, Communists and Socialists were being called traitors, Chaplin refused to turn against his friends.

Chaplin's liberal beliefs made him a number of powerful enemies in the United States. And his habit of keeping quiet, of refusing to respond to personal attack, only made his enemies more determined to ruin him.

Before *Modern Times* was released, rumors spread that the movie was a communist-inspired piece of propaganda. When the film opened, all the curious went to see if the rumors were true.

They laughed so hard they forgot to worry about the ideology. The reviewer for *The New Masses,* a Communist journal, applauded it wildly. But so did the reviewers of every other New York newspaper, including such conservative dailies as *The Evening Journal* and *Daily News.* Nevertheless, when the laughter died down, the suspicions remained. And when Chaplin announced that he was going to make a comedy about Hitler and Mussolini, the rumors flared anew.

It is important to note at this point that throughout most of the thirties, Hitler and Mussolini were not universally despised figures in the United States and England. The worldwide Depression had thrown governments all over the world into crisis. For example, French governments were chaotic and kept changing, and even in the United States, President Roosevelt's New Deal, with its trial-and-error methods, left some conservative thinkers frustrated. Italy and Germany had order, at least. The strong-arm methods of Der Führer and Il Duce had increased production and silenced radicals. Hitler and Mussolini had more than a few admirers in the democratic countries.

And those admirers didn't think much of Chaplin's making fun of the two fascist leaders. Fortunately, Chaplin was never one to launch or abandon projects according to pressures. He went ahead and made *The Great Dictator.*

Set in a country called Tomania, *The Great Dictator* follows the fortunes and misfortunes of two look-alikes—both played by Chaplin. One is a Jewish barber, and the other is the country's maniac dictator, Adenoid Hynkel. Hynkel is clearly Hitler, but instead of wearing the swastika, he wears a symbol consisting of two crosses (the double cross). He is just as anti-Jewish as Hitler, and just as power crazed. The thorn in Hynkel's side is Napoloni, the Mussolini-like dictator of Bacteria. Despite their rivalry, the fanatic Hynkel and buffoonish Napoloni plot to invade a nation called Austerlich. To dispel rumors of the invasion, Hynkel goes duck hunting on the day the invasion is scheduled.

Among the victims of Hynkel's persecution policies are the Jewish barber and his lovely friend, Hannah, a poor Jewish girl of the ghetto. Hynkel's men keep painting "Jew" on the walls of the barbershop, and the barber simply wipes off the word. The soldiers attack the ghetto and capture the barber, who is sent to a concentration camp. Hannah, however (played by Paulette Goddard), escapes.

On the day of the invasion of Austerlich, the barber breaks out of the concentration camp, and Dictator Hynkel falls out of his little fishing boat and swims to shore. The invasion of Austerlich occurs on schedule. Guards capture Hynkel, thinking him the barber. Other guards locate the barber and, thinking he is Hynkel, escort him to a podium where he—or, rather, Hynkel— is supposed to make a radio broadcast explaining to all Europe why the invasion is necessary.

No segment of any Chaplin film was more roundly criticized than the final speech made by the barber posing as Hynkel. Until that speech, *The Great Dictator* had been a very silly, very funny movie, in which two of the most powerful and terrifying men on earth were reduced to buffoonery. Perhaps the finest moment in the film comes when Hynkel, examining the globe and planning its conquest, removes it from its stand and does a beautiful, macabre dance with it. The globe becomes a balloon, a plaything, in Hynkel's hands, floating about at his will until—it pops!

In any case, farce is the mood of *The Great Dictator* until the barber-as-Hynkel makes his closing speech. The speech *is* incongruous, and yet understandably so. When Chaplin began *The Great Dictator* in 1939, Hitler had not yet demonstrated the extent of his evilness. He could still be made fun of. By the time the film was released, Europe was at war. Perhaps Chaplin felt that he had to make a final stab at convincing the world that peace was still possible—and congruity be damned if the job could be done.

"I'm sorry, but I don't want to be an emperor," the barber-as-Hynkel begins his final speech. He doesn't want to rule anyone; he wants to help everyone: "Jew, Gentile, black men, white." Indeed, he says, most human beings would rather help than hurt others. Greed, however, has poisoned men's souls; the speed and machinery of the modern era have been used by the greedy. "We think too much and feel too little. More than machinery we need humanity."

Despite the fact that greed has "goose-stepped us into misery and bloodshed," the barber continues, he believes that people must not despair. "The hate of men will pass and dictators die, and the power they took from the people will return to the people." But all must resist "these brutes—who despise you—enslave you . . . treat you like cattle and use you as cannon fodder." Soldiers must refuse to fight for slavery. Reminding his listeners that they have the power to create machines—that they are the masters and the machines the servants—the impassioned barber begs for world unity, in which all the world's little people can "do away with national barriers . . . do away with greed, with hate and intolerance. Let us fight for a world of reason—a world where science and progress will lead to the happiness of us all."

Chaplin's pleading notwithstanding, World War II came along anyway and plunged the earth into a violence the likes of which had never been known before.

Chaplin's marriage to Paulette Goddard, in contrast, ended quietly in 1942. The real bond between them—as Chaplin himself admitted—had been loneliness, not undying love. And after *Modern Times*, Paulette was too busy to be lonely. Unlike the first two Mrs. Chaplins, Paulette Goddard had talent as radiant as her beauty. Even before they started filming *The Great Dictator*, she and Chaplin were not seeing much of one another. However, their separation and divorce were handled without bitterness, and thereafter they had only kind things to say about each other.

During the late thirties, Chaplin grew ever closer to his two sons, Charles, Jr., and Sydney. Although he was a cool and proper person, not one to let his emotions show, Chaplin was a devoted parent who spent a great deal of time with the boys, helped them with their acting (both were interested in theater), and took them on trips. According to Charles, Jr., who wrote a book about his father, Chaplin was careful never to say an unpleasant word about their mother, Lita Grey, despite all the bitterness of the divorce. He also confided in them. Late in the decade, when it became clear that his marriage to Paulette Goddard would not last, he told his sons, according to Charles, Jr., "I'm not so sure I should ever marry. When I work I am oblivious to the world, and it's difficult to ask any woman to be happy when at times I forget her very existence." The boys were sorry to hear that; both of them were very fond of Paulette, who returned their feeling.

Despite his suspicion, Chaplin did marry again. Shortly after his divorce from Paulette, he wed Oona O'Neill, the eighteen-year-old daughter of the great American playwright Eugene O'Neill. Once again, part of the public was outraged: he was fifty-four, and she was a child. To make matters a bit more difficult, her father was bitterly against the match, and the public sympathized with him. To make matters much worse, at just about the time of his marriage, Chaplin was involved in a paternity suit. A young actress, Joan Barry, charged that Chaplin was the father of her child. Although a blood test determined that he was not the father, Chaplin was charged with violating the Mann Act—a federal statute that forbids a man from transporting a minor across state lines to have an affair with her. Attended by constant publicity, the case dragged on until 1945. The more serious charges were eventually dropped, but, incredibly (in view of the blood test results, which were not admitted during his trial), the court decided that Chaplin was the father, and therefore he had to pay for the child's upbringing.

During the war Chaplin joined a number of celebrities and lent support to the cause of "a second front." This was simply a campaign to persuade the United States to send troops into the Soviet Union to help the Russians turn back the German invaders. In the minds of his critics, his action was sure proof that Chaplin was a Communist.

After the war Chaplin made *Monsieur Verdoux,* and it may have been this movie that really put an end to whatever affection the American public still felt for him. *Monsieur Verdoux* tells the story of Henri Verdoux, a Frenchman devoted to his wife and son, who carries on a peculiar business: He meets wealthy women, marries them, and kills them for their money. He is very cold-blooded and scientific about it, and he carries on his business for many years. After his wife and son die, however, he gives himself up to the police. At his trial he admits his crimes but refuses to apologize for them. He is, he says, no different from the other men of his time—no different from the statesmen and politicians and munitions manufacturers who cold-bloodedly and scientifically plan and execute schemes that cause the deaths of millions. He is, by comparison, a small-time operator. That, of course, is the point of *Monsieur Verdoux*—that killing and evil itself are not only respectable but commonplace in modern society. Chaplin's Verdoux—well-groomed, well-mannered, very middle class—is a miniature version of society's destructive institutions.

Now, as then, critics disagree about *Monsieur Verdoux*. Some call it "Chaplin's mistake"; others are lavish in their praise. James Agee called it "one of the few indispensable works of our time." Chaplin himself thought it his best film. It is certainly his most serious.

One thing is certain: *Monsieur Verdoux* was not the movie Americans wanted to see in 1947. The Cold War hostility between America and Russia was beginning. An atmosphere of suspicion and fear was starting to envelop the country. The United States had not long before been victorious in a long, expensive war, and when international tension, rather than a sleepy peace, followed the struggle, Americans wanted someone to blame. At first it was enough to blame "the communists"—as if all the world's communists were a single, well-organized force. Then specific villains had to be found. People in the government started accusing colleagues of being communists. A California senator named Richard Nixon made a national reputation for himself by exposing—on flimsy and possibly faked evidence—a State Department official as a onetime member of the Communist Party. The Committee on Un-American Activities of the House of Representatives decided that the minds of the American people had been "poisoned" by Hollywood's legion of left-wing and Communist screenwriters; as a result of highly publicized hearings held in Washington, ten Hollywood writers were imprisoned for contempt of Congress—simply because they exercised their right to remain silent. (The Fifth Amendment of the U. S. Constitution says that no one can be forced to testify against himself. The "Hollywood Ten" went to jail because they refused to answer incriminating questions—although, in fact, they had a Constitutional right to refuse.) As the international situation worsened, so did the political climate. When the Soviet Union exploded an atomic bomb, Americans were told that traitors had sold the Russians atomic secrets. When the Communists won the revolution in China, Americans were told that traitors in the U. S. State Department had paved the way. When the Korean War started, many Americans believed that the conflict was the disruptive handiwork of disloyal people at home. Senator Joseph McCarthy of Wisconsin picked up the spirit of accusation and rode to national prominence, creating, en route, a climate of fear and distrust that touched every institution in the country. By the time the nightmare was over, thousands of jobs and reputations—and even two lives— were lost to hysteria; "black lists" told employers in many industries whom not to hire; and perhaps worst of all, people whose vocations were in education and entertainment—fields that are often related—were afraid to speak out. Controversy was to be avoided at all costs.

· Chaplin himself was continually harassed throughout the period. Immigration Department officials kept him busy with petty inquiries. Staff lawyers from the House Un-American Activities Committee questioned him about his political affiliations (although he was never called to testify at the actual HUAC hearings). The politically conservative American Legion picketed showings of his films and pressured exhibitors into refusing to show *Monsieur Verdoux*. Whenever Chaplin appeared in public, the barrage of questions came:

Are you a communist?
Why have you never become a citizen?
Have you ever committed adultery?
Why do you champion communist causes?

And always Chaplin answered simply, directly: he had no political affiliations; he neither championed nor loathed any form of government except fascism; yes, a friend of his might be a communist, but he was not in the habit of making or breaking friendships over political beliefs. He had never knowingly had an affair with another man's wife, and, besides, he was now a happily married man; the only woman in his life was his own wife.

He tried, as best he could, to ride out the storm. As had always been his habit, he escaped from his troubles by devoting himself to his work. The movie he made in this period, *Limelight*, was, considering the pressures he was under, surprisingly warm-hearted and optimistic. Released in 1952, *Limelight* tells a story close to Chaplin's heart: it is about an old, washed-up music-hall comedian in London. In a way it was about Chaplin—not the world-famous Charles Chaplin, but the Charles Chaplin who might have been, had there been no such thing as motion pictures.

After *Limelight* was shot, Chaplin, Oona, and their three children set out for a long trip to England. They sailed on the *Queen Elizabeth*, and on their second day at sea a cablegram arrived. Charles Spencer Chaplin was not to be permitted to reenter the United States. If he wished to apply for permission to reenter, he would have to go before a board of inquiry which would look into his political and moral beliefs.

Would it never end?

Yes, it would: the cablegram ended it. Chaplin was not about to subject himself to any more harassment. He was through with America.

Chaplin and Oona settled in Switzerland on a thirty-seven-acre estate overlooking Lake Geneva. Quiet and intelligent, shy but friendly, Oona was an ideal mate for Chaplin. She adored him and was determined to give him the sort of secure domestic life he had always longed for. She was also fiercely loyal: in response to her country's treatment of her husband, she renounced her United States citizenship. Altogether she and Chaplin had eight children; the youngest was born when Chaplin was in his seventies. Their son Michael has done some acting, but only their daughter Geraldine, so far, has made a career in motion pictures.

Outside of the United States, Chaplin made two movies. *A King in New York*, which has been called "maybe the worst movie ever made by a celebrated film artist," was released in England in 1957. It concerns a king who has to leave his country after a revolution; he goes to America, where, though he is penniless, he is able to live well simply because so many Americans are impressed with his royal blood. In 1966 Chaplin decided to direct another movie and let it be known that he wanted Marlon Brando and Sophia Loren to be the stars. They were, at the time, easily the most sought-after players in the movies. Both accepted Chaplin's offer without even reading the script. The movie, *A Countess from Hong Kong*, was not a great success, but it does contain some marvelously funny moments.

The Cold War cooled; the hysteria in the United States passed, and Charlie Chaplin grew old.

Almost all of us can think of an incident in our lives that brought out the worst in us. "Did *I* do *that*?" we ask ourselves, and since the answer is yes, the very thought of it embarrasses us. We would rather not even think of it again, though it was so awful that it is hard to forget. If we are intelligent and mature, however, we know that we learned a valuable lesson from that incident; we learned, if nothing else, not to make the same mistake again. Embarrassing as the memory of it may be, we know that that experience helped us to grow up.

Even countries grow up.

In 1972, twenty years after his departure, Charles Chaplin received a special invitation to return to the United States, and he agreed. No board of inquiry awaited him, no unfriendly reporters with hostile questions. The events of the past were on a lot of American minds, but they were an embarrassment. America had grown up, and in growing up it had learned what was really important about Charles Spencer Chaplin; he was greeted accordingly.

He returned, then, in triumph, a hero, a citizen of the world, a great artist, the "universal man of modern times."

124

17

Charlie's Back!

During the 1970s, Charles Spencer Chaplin received three no-table honors. Queen Elizabeth II of England knighted him, and he became Sir Charles. Two years before that, the Academy of Motion Picture Arts and Sciences had awarded him an Oscar—Hollywood's symbol of achievement. And a couple of months before that, the international film community had honored him by dedicating the Cannes Film Festival in France to him.

At the time, many people pointed out that these honors were long overdue—and indeed they were: Chaplin was in his eighties. But in a way they were all the more meaningful for coming so late. For although Chaplin's reputation as an artist had always been high, it took time before the extent of his artistry could be fully appreciated.

The brilliance of Chaplin's art was widely applauded in its heyday. Even before he had made his first feature-length film, he was recognized as the first great clown of the motion-picture screen. And writing of his wonderful pictures, critics did not hesitate to use such words as "masterpiece" and "work of art." Yet what people could not realize in the early years of the movies was that Chaplin's work would not only withstand the test of time but seem even more remarkable as time passed. Fifty years after the creation of Charlie the Tramp, Chaplin's place in film history had been strengthened rather than challenged. He remained not merely the first great clown, but the greatest of clowns. Critics in 1916, 1920, or 1928 could not realize how unique

Chaplin's genius was. None of them could write, as cinema historian Gerald Mast was able to write—with certainty—in 1973: "Charles Chaplin is the greatest film artist in motion picture history. He is to the movies what Shakespeare is to the drama."

In Europe Chaplin's movies had been showing with some consistency over the years. In the United States, however, they had not been so easy to see. Early in 1972, a group of movie lovers and Charlie Chaplin fans decided that it was high time that Americans of all ages should acquaint—and reacquaint—themselves with the Tramp. They got together and launched a Charlie Chaplin festival. First The Museum of Modern Art in New York held a special exhibition. In the museum's small cinema a selection of Chaplin's short films was shown, and in one of the galleries a display of still photographs pictured his long career. At the same time the company that owned the full-length features released them, and television stations began showing as many of the two-reelers as they could get their hands on.

The feature-length movies were shown first in a theater on Fifty-seventh Street in New York. Originally each film was to be shown for two weeks. However, the lines that formed outside the theater were so long, the enthusiasm of the patrons so great, that the movies had to be held over for a longer period of time. Interestingly, the crowds were larger in the second, third, and fourth weeks than they had been during the first. This is a sure sign that word of mouth, rather than advertising, is at work. People were telling their friends to go see the movies; sometimes they even brought friends and stayed themselves for a second or third viewing.

Then stories about Chaplin began to appear in newspapers and magazines. Thousands of Charlie Chaplin posters picturing the familiar image of the Tramp, usually leaning on his cane, his ankles crossed, were sold. There were Charlie Chaplin dolls and Charlie Chaplin coloring books and Charlie Chaplin wastepaper baskets. You could even buy a Charlie Chaplin sweatshirt. On the front of the sweatshirt was the head of the Tramp. On the back was the whole figure of the Tramp, photographed from behind. Above the rear image were two words: Charlie's Back!

As the films moved out of the theater on Fifty-seventh Street to make room for the next selection, they were exhibited in neighborhood theaters in New York and in theaters all across the country. It was 1914 all over again: Charlie Chaplin was sweeping the nation.

The climax of the Charlie Chaplin festival—and the event that more than any other made the American people aware of the Chaplin revival—occurred in April. It was the night of the Academy Awards, when the people of the Academy of Motion Picture Arts and Sciences get together to present the gold statuette called Oscar to the professionals among them who did the best work the year before. Academy Awards presentations are lavish, entertaining affairs televised into millions of homes. Usually the high point of the Academy Awards is the presentation of the Oscar for the best picture of the year. Because of its importance, this award is presented last. This year the presentation of the best-picture Oscar was not the high point of the show. After it was made, the lights in the big Hollywood theater dimmed, and a movie screen was lowered. A film began.

There on the screen was the Tramp. There was Charlie walking his famous waddle-walk, sliding, tripping, roller skating blindfolded, falling, dancing, boxing, sighing, hiccoughing. There was that familiar, funny figure, full of encouragement and hope for a rich drunkard who wants to kill himself, full of love for an abandoned little boy, a blind flower girl, a heart-hardened dance-hall girl. There he was, seasick, drunk, sick to his stomach, beaten up, chased by policemen, thrown in jail. There was the small, athletic, limber figure, capable of silly clumsiness and incredible gracefulness, doing the hysterically funny and touching things he did so uniquely in eighty movies. There was the man known the world around by his first name—Charlie, Charlot, Carlos, Carlino—still "the universal man of modern times."

Still Charlie: still the symbol of everyman, a man with whom ordinary people everywhere can identify. Still Charlie: a comic symbol of all the average folks who try to get along in a world that makes it not so easy to get along. His day-to-day struggle on film is familiar to people of all races and nationalities. Like them, he is powerless, poor, and good-hearted in a society ruled by the powerful, rich, and corrupt. He would rather be polite than rude, and he likes things that are beautiful better than things that are ugly. His main occupation is survival. He will do almost everything to survive, as long as he does not have to give up the only possessions he really cherishes: his freedom, his dignity, and his right to love.

The most wonderful thing about Charlie is that he does survive. Every day of his life on film he is set upon by forces more powerful than he. Landlords, bosses, waiters, police officers, other workingmen like himself—out to destroy him so that they can get his job, his share of the dinner, the woman he loves. And machines— machines that make him their servant when they work properly and machines that try to chew him up and swallow him when they do not work properly. But he survives. He survives and smiles. And he keeps his dignity and his belief in the beauty of life. Today he is betrayed; tomorrow he will be filled with trust. Now his heart is broken; later he will love again.

Because he never learns from his mistakes, Charlie is a constant victim of society. And yet he continues to believe in people and to love the smallest things that are beautiful in an ugly world. The people who are against him—the bosses and landlords and policemen—are never happy people in Chaplin's movies; they are grouchy and brutish and suspicious. In the conflicts of the moment, they are the winners and Charlie is the loser. But in the morning they will wake up needing another victim: their struggle to survive requires that they always find someone to pick on. Such a struggle never ends. Charlie will wake up in the morning, pick a flower, smell it, look at it, admire its beauty, put it through his buttonhole, and enjoy wearing it all day long. The flower will make him happy. Who, then, is the real victim of society? Happy Charlie or his miserable tormentors?

Still Charlie: and still Charlie lives. The little film in the Hollywood theater was proof of it. It lasted only about twelve minutes, and as it was being shown, the audience reacted exactly as they were meant to. Most of the time they were laughing —hard, hearty laughter that was continuous except for the few sections that showed the Tramp at a touching or melancholy moment. At those times the audience was hushed, only to be jarred a second later by some incredible bit of business that again filled the theater and the country with laughter. Considering the very high ratings of the Academy Awards telecast—over one hundred million people watched it—it is reasonable to say that during those twelve minutes all America was laughing.

The film made its point: Chaplin was a genius who could do as he pleased with the feelings of an audience. If he wanted people to laugh, he made them laugh. If he wanted them to stop laughing, he could accomplish that, too.

When the little movie ended and the lights came up again, the audience applauded. During the applause a white-haired man, eighty-three years old, walked out onto the stage. He was rather portly now, and he moved much more slowly than the Tramp. But it was Chaplin, all right. The slow, shy smile was the same; the sparkle in the clear, light eyes was still there. And when the people of the motion-picture profession saw him, they rose to their feet and clapped harder and shouted, "Bravo, Charlie!" and kept on clapping and cheering, and when he raised his hand asking them to stop, they cheered on, and on, and on.

So he stood there, waiting to receive his Oscar. It was not an Oscar for a best movie or a best performance, but an Oscar for a whole career in movies, an Oscar for the "incalculable effect he has had in making motion pictures the art form of this century." He stood and waited—Charlie Chaplin in Hollywood again—and the audience cheered and he smiled and his eyes filled with tears. He had been gone a long time and he was back.

Further Reading

Plenty of material is available to readers who would like to learn more about Charlie the Tramp, about the man who created him, and about Chaplin's importance in the history of motion pictures. The place to go is the public library, but you might also telephone the art museum in your city to find out if its library has a collection of books on the cinema. Every year more and more art museums are setting up film departments, and the people who work there are generally eager to help young film scholars.

Some of the best and most informative writing about Chaplin appears in books about the history of the cinema. Lewis Jacobs's *The Rise of the American Film* (Harcourt Brace Jovanovich, Inc., 1939) is one of the most readable of these books and explains very convincingly why Chaplin was such an important figure in the development of the art. Another fascinating book is *A Million & One Nights* (Simon & Schuster, Inc., paperback edition, 1964) by Terry Ramsaye. Originally published in 1926, this gigantic work—868 pages—gives a splendid picture of movies in the early years and features Chaplin as one of the five or six most brilliant stars.

It is always interesting to see what critics thought about movies when the movies were first shown. *American Film Criticism: From the Beginnings to "Citizen Kane"* (Liveright Publishing Corp., paperback, 1972), edited by Stanley Kauffmann and Bruce Henstell, contains reviews of Chaplin's major films from the

Keystone days, an appreciation of Chaplin written in 1917, and reviews of each of his feature-length films through *The Great Dictator*. In a few cases a favorable review is included along with a not-so-favorable review (although none of the reviews are really negative), and the comparison gives a splendid picture of the thinking of the times.

In 1949 James Agee wrote an article called "Comedy's Greatest Era" for the old *Life* magazine. A wonderful exploration of what made silent comedy so funny, this article can be read in *Agee On Film*, Volume I (Beacon Press, Inc., 1958), which also contains Agee's lavish praise for *Monsieur Verdoux*. "Comedy's Greatest Era" contrasts Chaplin's comedy with the comedy of Buster Keaton, Harold Lloyd, Laurel and Hardy, and other film comics, and contains a discussion of the importance of Mack Sennett.

The whole subject of comedy in motion pictures is analyzed at length in *The Comic Mind* by Gerald Mast (The Bobbs-Merrill Co., Inc., 1973). Although the book is thorough and readable, it is not intended for youngsters. Good readers, however, might want to take a look at the three chapters on Chaplin, which examine the anatomy of Chaplin's humor and explain exactly what it is that makes Charlie so funny.

Focus on Chaplin (Prentice-Hall, Inc., 1971), edited by Donald W. McCaffrey, is a collection of essays about Chaplin by various critics and scholars—some written long ago, some recently.

Chaplin's art has been the subject of several worthwhile books. *Chaplin: Last of the Clowns* (Vanguard Press, Inc., 1947) is probably the most complete analysis of the psychological makeup of the Tramp ever written. The author, Parker Tyler, was one of the first serious scholars of the cinema, and his seriousness is reflected in the book, which is recommended to only the very best readers: it is quite difficult. *The Great God Pan* by Robert Payne (Heritage House, 1952) is easier, but it is a little far-fetched at times. Still, this book, which places Chaplin in perspective with all the great clowns of mythology and history, is fun to read. *Charlie Chaplin, Early Comedies* by Isabel Quigley (E. P. Dutton & Co., Inc., 1968) is a delight; it contains short, colorful summaries of Chaplin's best films from the first through *Sunnyside*. Quigley's final statement, although it does not reduce the value of the book, might be argued with: "It is this early Charlie most people mean when they say Chaplin." Most other writers seem to think that Chaplin's greatest work was done between *A Dog's Life* and *Modern Times*. *The Little Fellow* by Peter Cotes and Thelma Niklaus (Citadel Press, revised edition, 1965) is a handy, informal book that discusses Chaplin's life in part one and his work in part two.

If you want to own one book about Chaplin, perhaps *The Films of Charlie Chaplin* (Citadel Press, paperback, 1965), by Gerald D. McDonald, is the one to choose—especially if you have seen a few of Chaplin's films. One of the beauties of Chaplin's work is the fact that once you have seen Charlie in action, you can visualize him in a variety of different circumstances. This big book does not shed much light on Chaplin's artistic development, but it contains summaries of each and every Chaplin film and brief excerpts from reviews, and it is crammed with pictures. As you read the summaries, you find yourself chuckling over bits of business that you haven't even seen. And then of course it's interesting, when you do get the opportunity to see the films, to compare the reality to what you imagined.

The two best books about Chaplin and his work are Theodore Huff's *Charlie Chaplin* (Arno Press, 1971 reprint of a 1951 work) and Roger Manvell's *Chaplin* (Little, Brown and Company, 1974). Both are complete biographies, written by two of the most widely respected film historians in the world.

Depending on what you're looking for, Chaplin's own *My Autobiography* (Simon & Schuster, Inc., 1964; paperback edition Pocket Books, 1966) will either delight or disappoint you. It is very long—560 pages in the paperback edition—and it contains a great deal about Charles and not so much about Charlie. The first five chapters, dealing with his dreadful London childhood, are touching and wonderful. Thereafter, Chaplin tells us perhaps a little more than we want to know about some aspects of his life—his travels, the many famous people he met—and not as much as we would like to know about others—he barely mentions his children, and he says too little about his wives and other people close to him; even his brother Sydney remains somewhat distant. There isn't much at all about moviemaking or about the people he worked with. (For example, Rolland Totheroh, who was Chaplin's cameraman from 1915 until 1947, isn't even mentioned; nor are many of the players Chaplin worked with throughout his career.) Moreover, Chaplin is somewhat neglectful of dates, and the reader sometimes has trouble placing certain events in their proper times. Nevertheless, *My Autobiography* is well worth reading, for it does the one thing that a good autobiography must do: read cover to cover, it gives the reader the feeling he knows the author and the way his mind works.

Chaplin is one of the great artists of the twentieth century; like most great artists he will be studied, appreciated, evaluated, and reevaluated for years and years to come. It may be that his real contribution to his era and to world history will not be precisely measurable until much more time has passed. When that time does come, when a yet-to-be-born historian sits down to write the truly authoritative biography of the man and an analysis of his work, he will of course draw much information from the books that have been written in Chaplin's lifetime. But he will spend less time reading than he will spend looking. For the genius of Charles Chaplin, like the genius of all great artists, is expressed best in the work itself. And the best way to understand Chaplin's genius is to look at his movies. That is true now, and it will be true a hundred years from now.

The silent little figure whose genius was discovered by children and who became "the most familiar human figure in the world," will continue to entertain people, and make people laugh, and touch and inspire people long after the man who played the part is gone. Thanks to film—the art form that Charles Chaplin helped to make an art form—and thanks to whatever it is that makes human beings love to laugh, Charlie Chaplin will never die.

Filmography

Some day, probably, all of the world's great movies will be transferred to video-tape cassettes, and most homes will have television sets equipped to play the cassettes. When that day comes, seeing a Charlie Chaplin movie will be easy: you'll be able to buy a copy and play it as readily as you buy and play a record.

Until then it's not so easy. True, Chaplin's short films are shown on television fairly regularly, and his features are exhibited periodically in theaters in big cities. For real Charlie Chaplin fans, though, this isn't enough. There's no sure way to get a bigger dose of Chaplin, except by renting his films—and that can be expensive. But there are things you can try.

Find out if the public library in your town has a film collection. Many libraries are beginning to lend or rent motion pictures as well as books and records.

Some schools nowadays have film clubs. If enough students are seriously interested in seeing old movies, your school may be persuaded to start such a club. The school probably owns a 16mm projector; all of Chaplin's short films can be rented in 16mm. Many of the films are also available in 8mm, at a much lower rental, for showings at home. (Projectors can also be rented.) To find out where to rent the films, look up "Motion Picture Film Libraries" in the classified section of your local telephone book.

The short films are also available to television. Write to your local stations—especially the public or educational station in your area—and ask them to inform you when they expect to televise Chaplin movies. Most stations are glad to hear from viewers, and your interest may even prompt them to schedule the films.

At the present time Chaplin's feature-length movies are shown only in theaters. If you live in a big city, check the movie listings in your newspapers, and within a year's time you can probably see most of them. If you live in a smaller city or town, tell the managers of your local theaters that you would like to see the Chaplin films. If enough of your friends and their parents make the same request, you have a better chance of persuading the theater managers that it is time for your own local Charlie Chaplin festival.

A list of all of Chaplin's movies, some with release dates, follows.

Keystone Comedies (1914)

Making a Living
Kid Auto Races at Venice
Mabel's Strange Predicament
Between Showers
A Film Johnnie
Tango Tangles
His Favorite Pastime
Cruel, Cruel Love
The Star Boarder
Mabel at the Wheel
Twenty Minutes of Love
Caught in a Cabaret
Caught in the Rain
A Busy Day
The Fatal Mallet
Her Friend the Bandit
The Knockout
Mabel's Busy Day
Mabel's Married Life
Laughing Gas
The Property Man

The Face on the Barroom Floor
Recreation
The Masquerader
His New Profession
The Rounders
The New Janitor
Those Love Pangs
Dough and Dynamite
Gentlemen of Nerve
His Musical Career
His Trysting Place
Tillie's Punctured Romance
Getting Acquainted
His Prehistoric Past

Essanay Comedies

His New Job (1915)
A Night Out
The Champion
In the Park
The Jitney Elopement

The Tramp
By the Sea
Work
A Woman
The Bank
Shanghaied
A Night in the Show
Carmen (1916)
Police (1916)
Triple Trouble (1918)

Mutual Comedies

The Floorwalker (1916)
The Fireman
The Vagabond
One A.M.
The Count
The Pawnshop
Behind the Screen
The Rink
Easy Street (1917)
The Cure
The Immigrant
The Adventurer

First National Films

A Dog's Life (1918)
The Bond
Shoulder Arms
Sunnyside (1919)

A Day's Pleasure
The Kid (1921)
The Idle Class
Pay Day (1922)
The Pilgrim (1923)

United Artists

A Woman of Paris (1923)
The Gold Rush (1925)
The Circus (1928)
City Lights (1931)
Modern Times (1936)
The Great Dictator (1940)
Monsieur Verdoux (1947)
Limelight (1952)

Independently produced

A King in New York (1957)

Directed by Charles Chaplin:

A Woman of Paris (1923)
A Countess from
    Hong Kong (1967)

These were the only films directed by Chaplin but not starring Chaplin. Chaplin did, however, make brief appearances in both movies—in both cases as a porter.

Index

Index

Picture Acknowledgments

Grateful acknowledgment is made for photographs which appear through the courtesy of The Museum of Modern Art, Film Stills Department; Cinemabilia, New York; Universal Pictures; and United Press International, New York and Los Angeles.

The commercial distributor of Chaplin's films is Columbia Pictures, Inc., New York. The nontheatrical distributor of all available Chaplin movies is RBC Films, Los Angeles.

Format by Kohar Alexanian
Set in 11 pt. Modern No. 21
Composed printed and bound by The Haddon Craftsmen, Inc.
HARPER & ROW, PUBLISHERS, INCORPORATED